YEAR 'ROUND ACTIVITIES FOR THREE-YEAR-OLD CHILDREN

Preschool Curriculum Activities Library

YEAR 'ROUND ACTIVITIES FOR THREE-YEAR-OLD CHILDREN

Anthony J. Coletta, Ph.D.

Associate Professor of Early Childhood Education
William Paterson College, Wayne, New Jersey

Kathleen Coletta

Illustrated by Margie Tuohy Jordan

THE CENTER FOR APPLIED RESEARCH IN EDUCATION INC., WEST NYACK, NEW YORK

*To our parents: Rae, Greg, Margaret, and Enrico,
who have always supplied us with
a boundless amount of love and support*

Library of Congress Cataloging-in-Publication Data

Coletta, Anthony J.
    Year 'round activities for three-year-old children.

    (Preschool curriculum activities library)
    1. Education, Preschool—Curricula—Handbooks,
manuals, etc.   2. Perceptual-motor learning—Handbooks, manuals, etc.   3. Play—Handbooks, manuals,
etc.   4. Creative activities and seat work—Handbooks,
manuals, etc.   I. Coletta, Kathleen.   II. Title.
III. Coletta, Anthony J. Preschool curriculum
activities library.
LB1140.4.C643   1986   372.19   85-26998

ISBN 0-87628-982-0

Printed in the United States of America

ABOUT THE AUTHORS

Anthony J. Coletta, Ph.D., is presently associate professor of Early Childhood Education at William Paterson College (Wayne, New Jersey), where he teaches Early Childhood Education courses. The holder of a Montessori teaching certificate, Dr. Coletta has taught at all levels, preschool to junior high, working with both gifted and learning disabled preschool and primary children.

Kathleen Coletta, B.A., Early Childhood Education, is an experienced preschool teacher and currently serves as the Director of the Ponds Valley Preschool in Oakland, New Jersey. She has also served as a consultant to other area preschools developing curriculum manuals, newsletters, and a parent-education program.

ACKNOWLEDGMENTS

We thank . . .

. . . **Margie Tuohy Jordan** for painstakingly reviewing each activity so that our ideas could be accurately depicted in her drawings. We also appreciate her creative suggestions.

. . . **Michelle Lyons** for typing all three manuscripts with accuracy, efficiency, and patience.

. . . **Donna Reid and the staff** of the Donna Reid Child Development Center, Franklin Lakes, New Jersey, for encouraging and implementing our curriculum plan as it was developed and giving us continuous feedback, criticisms, and suggestions. The teachers who cooperated during the field testing were Kathy Tenkate, Linda Fitzsimmons, Lois Wallace, Lori Doda, Rose Silvestri, and Emily Lio.

. . . **Bob Messano** for his original songs.

. . . **John Sheehan and Kevin DeFreest** for their musical arrangements.

. . . **Faith Geruldsen, LeAnn Bucco, and Dawn Ciarleglio,** graduate students at William Paterson College, Wayne, New Jersey, for assisting with the research of books, fingerplays, records, and poetry that enhanced our curriculum and for contributing their own teaching ideas.

. . . **William Strader,** doctoral candidate in early childhood education at the University of Massachusetts, Amherst, Massachusetts, for contributing many suggestions based on his extensive experience as a preschool teacher and director.

. . . **Alpha Caliandro,** associate professor of early childhood education at William Paterson College, for guiding our selections of classical music pieces recommended in the activities.

. . . **Dr. Laura Aitken, Dr. Marge Moreno, and Joan Heins,** faculty of Early Childhood Education at William Paterson College, for their astute observations and recommendations regarding parts of the manuscript.

We further wish to acknowledge those traditional nursery rhymes, action songs, and fingerplays for which no authors have been located and that appear in many other books.

CHARACTERISTICS OF THREE-YEAR-OLDS

The third year of life is a time of expansion for children's cognitive, affective, and physical growth. Three-year-olds are more conforming and predictable than two-year-olds and tend to show curiosity toward anything new in their environment. Fifty percent of their play is sensory-motor,* resulting in a strong need for activities that develop fine and gross motor abilities. The spoken language of early three-year-olds may consist of about 900 words and increases to 1500 by the age of four.**

Three-year-olds are capable of magical thinking—that is, the belief that their actions and thoughts can bring about events. This egocentric and attractive feature of three-year-olds (as well as four-year-olds and five-year-olds) allows them to create a life of fantasy and make-believe. Stuffed animals can take on human characteristics (animism), providing children the opportunity for development of imagination and language.

The ability to think symbolically has increased at this age. Typically, three-year olds might take two dominoes, stand them up, and pronounce, "This is my mommy and daddy!" Artwork is often exhibited by later three-year-olds as a face with stick arms and legs.

Three-year-olds can speak in sentences of four, six, or more words, listen to short stories, and rote count to ten or more. They can often identify as many as seven colors and use scissors (although lines may not be followed accurately).

These and many other characteristics are classified under the areas of cognition, language, self, social studies, math, science, and gross and fine motor movements, and they are listed in the Skills–Concepts Checklist for Three-Year-Olds. These seventy-nine skills and concepts are sequentially presented and systematically developed in the children through carefully planned activities for September through June.

Using this book will save you a significant amount of time that would normally be allotted to short- and long-term curriculum planning. More important, the time you spend teaching children will be used more effectively. Please refer to the following section for specific suggestions for using this book, the Checklist, and the activities.

* Charles F. Wolfgang, *Growing and Learning Through Play.* (New York: McGraw-Hill, 1981).
** Margaret Lay-Dopyera and John Dopyera, *Becoming a Teacher of Young Children,* 2nd ed. (Lexington, Mass.: D. C. Heath, 1982).

SKILLS-CONCEPTS CHECKLIST*
FOR THREE-YEAR-OLDS
(Developmental Characteristics)

A child who is 36 to 48 months of age continues to expand his or her cognitive, affective, and physical growth. The following abilities will emerge as the child approaches age four. The activities within this book have been designed to develop the skills and concepts listed below in a manner consistent with the child's needs and interests. Monitor the child's progress and evaluate it twice during the school year by placing a check (√) next to the skill or concept once it has been mastered.

Name _____ Birthdate _____

COGNITIVE

Personal Curiosity/Autonomy	JAN.	JUNE
1. Shows curiosity and the need to investigate/explore anything new		
2. Asks questions (Who?, What?, Where?, or Why?)		

Senses		
3. Demonstrates accurate sense of touch, smell, and taste		
4. Identifies common sounds		
5. Places objects on their outlines		
6. Observes objects closely		

Memory		
7. Recalls three objects that are visually presented		
8. Identifies what's missing from a picture		
9. Acts out simple everyday activities		

Logical Thinking		
10. Places three pictured events from a familiar story in sequence and expresses each picture sequence in three thoughts		

Relationships		
11. Pairs related objects and pictures, such as shoe and sock		
12. Recognizes which doesn't belong in a group of three items (for example, banana, chair, and apple)		

Creativity		
13. Draws a face with facial parts and stick arms and legs		
14. Dramatizes a simple story		
15. Uses animistic thinking (stuffed animals have human characteristics)		
16. Plays using symbols (objects stand for real objects)		

Comments: _____

_____

* This checklist was developed from the *Skill-Concept Development Checklists for Two Through Five Year Olds* (St. Louis County, Missouri: Parent-Child Early Education). Developed by the Ferguson-Florissant School District. Parts reprinted with their permission.

LANGUAGE

Sentence Structure

	JAN.	JUNE
17. Speaks in four- to six-word sentences		
18. Uses *I, you, me, he,* and *she* correctly		
19. Engages in simple conversation		
20. Memorizes and repeats simple rhymes, songs, or fingerplays of four lines		
21. Understands sentences and questions as indicated by a relevant response		
22. Names plural form to refer to more than one		
23. Describes action in pictures		

Listening

	JAN.	JUNE
24. Listens to short stories and simple poems		
25. Follows two directions		
26. Understands opposites (up/down; open/closed; stop/go; happy/sad; fast/slow; hot/cold)		
27. Understands prepositions (in, out, over, under, on, off, top, bottom, in front of, in back of)		

Labeling

	JAN.	JUNE
28. Names concrete objects in environment		
29. Recognizes and names articles of clothing worn		
30. Recognizes and names pieces of furniture		

Comments: _____

_____

_____

SELF

	JAN.	JUNE
31. Points to and names body parts (head, hands, arms, knees, legs, chin, feet, and face parts)		
32. Tells own full name, sex, and age		
33. Feels good about self and abilities		

Comments: _____

_____

_____

SOCIAL STUDIES

Interpersonal

	JAN.	JUNE
34. Enjoys being with other children		
35. Begins learning the give and take of play		
36. Begins participation in a group		

Concepts

	JAN.	JUNE
37. Begins to understand that self and others change		
38. Understands that parental figures care for home and family		
39. Understands that people are alike and different in how they look and feel (3½ to 4)		

Comments: _____

_____

_____

MATH

Counting	JAN.	JUNE
40. Rote counts to ten		
41. Understands number concepts (when presented with a given number of objects, child can tell how many there are up to six)		

Classifying		
42. Sorts objects into two given categories (by size, shape, or color)		

Size Differences		
43. Understands concepts of full and empty		
44. Understands big/little; tall/short		

Shapes		
45. Points to and labels shapes		
46. Matches shapes (circle, square, triangle, and rectangle)		

Sets		
47. Matches sets containing up to five objects		
48. Constructs sets of blocks when given a model		

Comments: _____

_____

_____

_____

SCIENCE

Concepts		
49. Understands that there are many kinds of animals		
50. Understands that animals move in different ways		
51. Understands that most plants make seeds for new plants		
52. Understands that seeds grow into plants with roots, stems, leaves, and flowers		
53. Understands that air is everywhere		
54. Understands that water has weight		

Colors		
55. Matches colors		
56. Points to appropriate color upon command		
57. Names three primary colors (red, yellow, and blue)		

Comments: _____

_____

_____

_____

GROSS MOTOR

Arm–Eye Coordination		
58. Catches a large ball from 5- to 8-foot distance		
59. Throws a ball overhand with accuracy from 4- to 6-foot distance		
60. Rolls a large ball to a target		
61. Throws a beanbag at a target five feet away		

Body Coordination	JAN.	JUNE
62. Walks forward/backward on an 8-foot line		
63. Jumps three jumps with both feet		
64. Hops on one foot two or more times		
65. Moves body in response to simple teacher commands		
66. Walks on tiptoe		
67. Rides a tricycle		
68. Claps with music		

Comments:

_____

_____

_____

_____

FINE MOTOR

Finger Strength and Dexterity

69. Makes balls and snakes with clay		
70. Pastes with index finger		

Eye-Hand Coordination

71. Strings at least four half-inch beads		
72. Puts pegs into pegboard		
73. Screws and unscrews nuts, bolts, and lids of various sizes		
74. Holds crayon with fingers rather than fist		
75. Paints with a large brush on large piece of paper		
76. Copies horizontal lines, vertical lines, circles, crosses, diagonal lines		
77. Uses scissors but does not necessarily follow lines		
78. Puts together a six- or seven-piece puzzle		
79. Laces following a sequence of holes		

Comments:

_____

_____

_____

_____

ABOUT THE
PRESCHOOL CURRICULUM ACTIVITIES LIBRARY

Year 'Round Activities for Three-Year-Old Children is the second volume of three in the *Preschool Curriculum Activities Library.* This *Library* represents a multisensory developmental approach to curriculum development for two-, three-, and four-year-old children. The activities presented stimulate the senses of sight, touch, hearing, smell, and taste, while being appropriate to the children's stages of development. Several important research models provide a foundation for creative lesson plans that help you solve the major organizational problem in early childhood education—matching developmentally appropriate daily activities to traditional preschool topics.

In this *Library*, the major work of building a preschool curriculum has been done for you. Topics, skills, and concepts that have been "matched" to the proper stage of the child's growth are included in all the activities. Topics in the form of themes and subthemes have been carefully identified and ordered and are based on seasonal interest. A total of 585 activities are described in the three-book *Library*, and each one is based on skills identified in the Checklists for two-, three-, and four-year-old children.

More important, each book of the *Preschool Curriculum Activities Library* has been field tested to provide you with a complete developmental program. In addition, **Developmental Skills-Concepts Checklists*** are included for this age group as well as the other two age groups in the *Library*. (See the Complete Preschool Development Plan at the back of the book.) Each Checklist is an individual skills record that outlines the abilities you can reasonably expect from children at each age.

The following uses are recommended for the preceding Skills-Concepts Checklist for Three-Year-Olds found on pages viii–xi:

- Assess a child's skill and concept ability levels. This information of children's strengths and/or deficiencies can help modify curriculum plans by creating or changing activities.
- Monitor a child's progress throughout the year. Duplicate the Checklist for each child and keep it in his or her folder. Supplement the Checklist evaluations with anecdotal statements. It is recommended that the Checklist be completed twice yearly, in January and June.
- Use the Checklist as a progress report to parents and as a reference during parent conferences. Specific statements rather than broad generalizations can be made. Parents who are concerned about skill-concept development will be assured that their children will not miss any major topics, concepts, or skills.
- Use to individualize instruction by grouping children with a common strength or weakness. Teaching one lesson to a small group needing similar skill development saves the teacher's time and energy.
- Give the Checklist to the child's teacher next year. He or she will then know what skills the child has been exposed to and can more easily plan reinforcement and extension.

*The Skills-Concepts Checklist was originally developed by Dr. Walter Hodges of Georgia State University, Atlanta, Georgia, while he was working as a consultant with the Ferguson-Florissant schools in Ferguson, Missouri. The Checklist has been further modified by the authors to include the findings of other early childhood authorities, notably Dr. Carol Seefeldt, *A Curriculum for Preschools,* 2nd ed. (Columbus, O.: Chas. E. Merrill, 1980); Dr. Joseph Sparling, *Learningames for the First Three Years* (New York: Walker and Co., 1979); and Dr. Charles F. Wolfgang, *Growing and Learning Through Play* (New York: McGraw-Hill, 1981).

- Use the Checklist to understand the total development of children as they pass through the preschool years. The Checklist can also be used for inservice training, parent workshops, or orienting new staff members.
- Use a checkmark (√) to keep track of those skills mastered by the children. With this simple checking system, you can quickly scan the Checklist, noting the skills and concepts required. These skills and concepts can be reinforced as part of routine activities as you desire.

Each skill or concept has been carefully integrated into the curriculum. You know that the differences among two-, three-, and four-year-olds are more impressive than among seven-, eight-, and nine-year-olds. The Checklist provides a justification for creating differentiated learning experiences with classes of two-, three-, and four-year-olds. It can easily be reproduced for use in individual record keeping, as a progress report to parents, and as a tool for individualizing instruction.

Monthly themes and weekly subthemes of high interest are included as part of a unit approach to curriculum development. Within the unit framework, an entire preschool can study a broad topic for one month, separated into four related areas or weekly subthemes. The five activities within each subtheme are organized to develop and reinforce the skills and concepts found on the Skills-Concepts Checklist.

The ten themes and thirty-nine subthemes, one for each month and week of the school year, were created with the following concepts in mind:

1. Learning begins with the selection of topics that are most familiar to children and gradually expands into areas that are more challenging.
2. Good teaching involves creative long- and short-range planning. Within a well-organized framework, teachers can follow the child's lead and expand on his or her interests.
3. A thematic approach to curriculum development is most effective when the themes are highly related to the immediate environment surrounding the child.

Every effort has been made to connect topics to the seasonal events children will see and hear about each month. While this is not a holiday curriculum, some holidays are included in the subthemes and activities. For example, the November theme, "Home and Family," is strongly related to the meaning of Thanksgiving. Religious holidays, however, are not included within the themes and subthemes. Such holidays should be observed by each school in a manner appropriate to local cultural traditions.

195 ready-to-use activities are described for an entire school year of thirty-nine weeks (or ten months). Along with a multisensory emphasis, many physical movement suggestions are included to help children explore each topic as an active participant, at his or her own pace.

The activities can be used either with a whole group or in small groups. Whenever possible, you should aim to accomplish the activities in small groups or individually. Each activity, one for each day of the school year, includes the skill or concept to be learned, behavioral objectives, materials needed, a step-by-step procedure, and ways to vary or extend the activity.

Each of the thirty-nine subthemes contains five activities selected from the subject areas described here. Read the activities before trying them, so that materials such as books, records, posters, puzzles, and other recommended resources can be located or ordered, and the activities can be modified to best meet the needs of the children you teach.

By using these activities as a springboard, you can create challenging and involving activities that can be easily integrated into any existing educational framework.

The following subject areas are covered in the *Preschool Curriculum Activities Library*:

Language Arts. The language arts activities in this curriculum follow a language experience approach. The children's receptive and expressive language is enhanced through the use of fingerplays, nursery rhymes, poetry, discussions, and experience charts. Furthermore, many fine books for children are suggested, including Caldecott Medal and Honor books.

There are no formal reading or writing experiences among the 195 activities. Such experiences are appropriate for the concrete stage of development, ages seven to eleven. Stimulating experiences, along with the manipulation of objects, are much more important for preschoolers than ditto sheets and workbook activities.

Science. The science activities are aimed at encouraging observation, comparison, exploration, testing, inquiry, and problem solving. Within many activities, children's senses are stimulated. You can help them notice cause and effect, as well as keep simple records.

Nutrition/Foods Experience. With the nutrition activities, children learn about group cooperation, weights and measures, time, and changes of matter from one form to another. Moreover, they develop an understanding of how to follow directions in sequence, gain pleasure from creating simple foods, and develop good eating habits.

Creative Dramatics/Movement. Creative dramatics aid children in developing language and spontaneous play. Creative dramatics can take many forms, such as creative movement (in which children use sensory-motor abilities and gain skill in body control), rhythm, tempo, timing, following directions, and group cooperation. While involved in creative dramatics, children sometimes use concrete objects as symbols, and you can extend their play to include pantomime, story dramatizations, role playing, and puppetry.

Social Studies. The social studies activities focus on learning about self, home, family, transportation, and the immediate as well as the larger community. Emphasis is on the children's involvement in their own learning. Therefore, field trips to local sites are an important part of the curriculum. The Variations/Ways to Extend sections of several lessons suggest inviting parents and other community people into the classroom to share their special talents and information.

Art. Art for preschoolers is a creative process that allows for choice, exploration, and imaginative expression in a pleasant, supportive atmosphere. Each child's work should be unique and recognizably different from another's. These process goals are best reached through traditional preschool techniques such as painting at an easel, finger painting, and rolling and molding clay.

The art experiences suggested in the *Library* are tied to particular curriculum topics. In this sense, the art activities are limited in their potential for pure, creative experience because they have been suggested as ways to reinforce certain ideas for the children. Keeping in mind that any activity described in this book is meant to be only *one* experience in a whole week of related activities, you must be certain to provide the children with plenty of pure art activities at other times. Opportunities for exploring color, line, and form and for discovering the effects of various media on different surfaces in an open-ended fashion will allow each child to make a personal statement with art.

Exposure to beautiful works of art can enhance the classroom environment. A number of activities include suggestions for obtaining inexpensive, high-quality color reproductions from the National Gallery of Art. These have special appeal for young children, such as the work of Renoir and Matisse.

Music. The goals of the music experiences are to develop appreciation, participation, and responsiveness; musical competencies such as listening, performance, rhythm, and creativity; and musical concepts such as pitch, volume, and contrasts. Many recorded songs are suggested along with new original music specifically designed for this curriculum. In addition, certain classical pieces that provide stimulating background music and exposure to the works of great composers are recommended.

Math. The math activities attempt to reflect the needs of the preoperational child, ages two to seven. Opportunities are presented that allow children to learn through direct experiences such as sorting, comparing, and ordering. Playful lessons develop skills in rote counting, numeral recognition, and sets. Again, duplicated sheets are not utilized in any of the math activities because they are a semiconcrete rather than a concrete vehicle for learning.

Thinking and Gross Motor Games. The thinking games motivate children to develop cognitive skills within a play situation. When involved in a thinking game, children are learning to identify, classify, and apply skills.

Gross motor games contribute to positive physical and mental health by strengthening muscles and helping to free children from tension. Social development is aided when the children cooperate and learn the positions of leader and follower. Finally, self-concepts are enhanced as youngsters acquire motor skills and feelings of success and enjoyment.

A Complete Preschool Development Plan consisting of the three Checklists is included at the end of each book. This Plan displays the developmental skills progression for two-, three-, and four-year-olds, giving you a clear picture of the prekindergarten skills children can be expected to develop. While educators know that learning is uneven (that is, a child who is three may not necessarily demonstrate all the three-year-old skills), the Plan gives you an overall idea of how normal development progresses and a place to start in assessing children's development. It also serves as a visual presentation of the cognitive theory that ideas grow from concrete to abstract and from simple to complex as the child learns and grows.

The three books in the *Library* can be used independently or simultaneously by a school that has classes for two-, three-, and four-year-olds. The children can study the same topics but in ways that are of interest to and appropriate for their level of growth. This exciting concept can mobilize a school and encourage total involvement of students, teachers, and parents in learning—all working together to help the children develop and grow to their fullest potential.

Anthony J. Coletta
Kathleen Coletta

CONTENTS

MAY: COMMUNITY WORKERS 177

LEARNING ABOUT OURSELVES AND OTHERS

- ○ Getting to Know One Another
- ○ Self-Concept
- ○ Friends and School

II-1   SING AND BE HAPPY

Subject Area: Music

Concept/Skill: Memorizes and repeats a simple song

Objective: The children will become acquainted with the teacher and one another by learning to sing a song.

Material: • Words to song

Procedure:

1. Teach the song "If You're Happy and You Know It." Words and music can be found in *The Spectrum of Music* by M. Marsh (New York: Macmillan, 1980).

2. Later, introduce the action words. Begin with actions your students can perform while seated to encourage all of them to participate. Then substitute other action words and phrases that will bring the group to their feet, such as *stamp, jump,* and *reach up high.* Here are some sample verses:

    a. If you're happy and you know it sing with me.
       If you're happy and you know it sing with me.
       If you're happy and you know it then your face will surely show it.
       If you're happy and you know it sing with me.
    b. Tap your toe.
       c. Clap your hands.
         d. Shake your head.
           e. Wiggle your fingers.

Variations/Ways to Extend:

• Have the children use cymbals, sandblocks, shakers, rhythm sticks, bells, and other available instruments as they sing the song.

• Have the children draw easel paintings to show "I'm Happy!"

II-2   SUMMER FUN BOOKLET

Subject Area: Art

Concepts/Skills: Speaks in four- to six-word sentences
Uses "I" correctly
Holds crayon with finger rather than fist

Objectives: The children will tell about their summer experiences and create pictures to reflect their thoughts.

Materials: • Construction paper
• Crayons in variety of colors
• Stapler
• Items reminiscent of each child's summer

Procedure:

1. Ask the children to bring in a few special treasures (shells, feathers, pressed flowers, small stones) from their summer to share with the group.
2. Talk together about what makes summer different from the other seasons and so much fun.
3. Now let the children express their thoughts and feelings on construction paper with crayons. Then, either underneath the picture or on the back of the paper, write the story each child dictates about that particular picture.
4. Let the children draw as many pictures as they want.
5. Staple each child's pictures together, making a book about summer for each child to take home.

Variations/Ways to Extend:

• Let the children, using their collections of items, engage in set and sub-set play. Help them to sort by size, color, and shape into small containers.
• Help the children glue some of their special treasures onto a piece of colored mat board to form a "Summer Treasures" collage.

II-3 BRIGHT LIGHT ON ME

Subject Area: Social Studies

Concepts/Skills: Pastes on paper
Feels good about self
Understands that people are alike and different in how they look

Objective: The children will model for their individual silhouette pictures.

Materials:
- One sheet of 12″ × 18″ newsprint for each child
- One sheet of 12″ × 18″ black construction paper for each child
- Masking tape
- Projector or other bright light source
- Stapler
- Pencil
- Chair or stool
- White posterboard
- Scissors
- Rubber cement

Procedure:

1. Tape the newsprint on a wall at the level of the child's head.
2. Seat the child on a chair or stool, close to the wall.
3. Shine a bright light onto the child.
4. Carefully draw around the shadow created, including all the little details (curls, ribbons, cowlicks).

5. Staple the newsprint silhouette onto black construction paper.
6. Cut out both sheets and discard the newsprint.
7. Carefully dot rubber cement on the back of the black silhouette and paste onto the white posterboard. (You might have the child do this part of the activity under your supervision. Be sure the child does not inhale the rubber cement's fumes.)
8. After discussing and pointing out differences in features, allow each child to pick out his or her own silhouette.

Variations/Ways to Extend:
- Make a bulletin board display of all the children's silhouettes.
- Read *Little Chicken* by Margaret Wise Brown (New York: Harper and Row, 1982).

II-4   I AM ME

Subject Area: Language Arts

Concepts/Skills: Repeats fingerplay
Uses "I" correctly
Points to and names body parts

Objective: The children will learn a new fingerplay using the word *I*.

Material: • Words to the fingerplay

Procedure:

1. Teach the following words to the fingerplay and demonstrate the actions:

> I touch my head,
> I touch my toes,
> I shake my hands,
> I touch my nose!
> I fold my arms,
> I cross my feet,
> I nod two times,
> I take a seat.

2. Repeat this fingerplay several times, using additional actions.

Variations/Ways to Extend:

- Read *Will I Have a Friend?* by Miriam Cohen (New York: Macmillan, 1971).
- Have the children verbally fill in a "My 'I' Book" while you print in the responses. Each page should have a different statement and illustration. Some suggestions are: I love————. I have fun when I ———— . I want to ———— . I really don't like to ———— .

II–5 WHO'S THAT TAPPING AT THE WINDOW?

Subject Area: Music

Concepts/Skills: Memorizes and repeats a simple song of four lines
Asks questions
Appreciates and participates in music

Objective: The children will learn one another's names through the song.

Material: • Words to "Who's That Tapping at the Window?"

Procedure:

1. Sit on the floor and sing the following song quietly with the children. The words and music may be found in *This Is Music for Kindergarten and Nursery School* by A. McCall (Boston: Allyn and Bacon, 1967):

   Who's that tap-ping at the win-dow?
   Who's that knock-ing at the door?
   John-ny's tap-ping at the win-dow.
   Tam-my's knock-ing at the door.

2. Have the children listen for their names and then tap the floor on the word *tapping* or knock loudly on the word *knocking*.

Variations/Ways to Extend:

• Ask each child to stand, one at a time, and have the whole group sing the song to that child. Ask the child standing to pantomime the actions.
• Demonstrate to the children how to ask questions, such as "What is your favorite food?" "What is your favorite color?" "What is your favorite toy?" Encourage the children to ask questions of one another.

II-6 NAME MOSAIC

Subject Area: Art

Concepts/Skills: Applies glue and pastes collage pieces
Refers to self by name
Becomes aware of printed name

Objective: The children will construct a mosaic of their names.

Materials:
- One large sheet of light-colored paper for each child
- Dark-colored crayon or marker
- Pre-cut small pieces of colored paper
- Paste or glue
- One 3-inch paper square for each child on which to put glue

Procedure:

1. Print each child's first name in block letters on a large piece of paper. Let the child watch you so he or she can understand that certain letters are used to form the name.
2. Give each child a pile of colored-paper scraps and a glue square.
3. Tell the child to fill in the letters of his or her name by pasting the small pieces of colored paper onto the letter outlines. Demonstrate and give additional directions as needed.
4. Talk about the work each child is doing, naming the letters and the colors. Praise each child's efforts.
5. Display each child's work when finished.

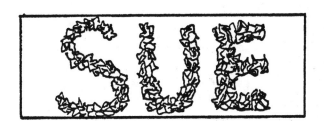

Variations/Ways to Extend:
- Use the mosaic as the cover for a book about the child. Fill the book with pictures of things he or she likes, such as favorite toys.
- Use colored aquarium stones instead of paper scraps to glue onto the letters. Be sure to use heavy cardboard for the base when using stones.
- Have the children decorate the words *Mommy* and *Daddy*. Frame these with black construction paper and let the children use them as gifts for their parents.

Weekly Subtheme: Self-Concept

II-7 MY STRAWBERRY ICE CREAM CONE

Subject Area: Math

Concept/Skill: Matches sets containing up to five objects

Objective: The children will match ice cream cones to matching sets of strawberry dots.

Materials:
- Five ice cream cones cut from brown posterboard
- Five scoops of ice cream cut from pink posterboard
- Brown and red markers
- Scissors

Procedure:

1. Use the brown marker to put dots on one side of each ice cream cone and corresponding numerals from 1 through 5 on the other side. Cut a slit in the top of the cone for the scoop to fit through. (See the illustrations here.)

2. Draw the corresponding number of dots on each scoop of ice cream with a red marker to represent strawberries.
3. Discuss with the children what their favorite ice cream flavors are.
4. Count the dots on each cone and have the children count along with you. Then count the dots on each scoop of ice cream.
5. Show the children how to match each scoop of ice cream to the appropriate cone.

Variations/Ways to Extend:

- Use the activity to teach numeral recognition. Have the children match the numerals to the corresponding number of dots on the ice cream scoops.
- Have the children paste circles and triangles on their own cones to take home. Ask them what number of strawberries they would like and guide them in making the correct number of dots.

II-8 AN ACTION SONG

Subject Area: Music

Concepts/Skills: Memorizes a four-line song
 Points to and names body parts

Objectives: The children will learn a song and demonstrate knowledge of body parts.

Material: • Tune of "Skip to My Lou"

Procedure:

1. While singing, do the actions of the song:

   Clap, clap, clap your hands, (*sing*)
   (action), (action), (action) your hands (*sing and do action*)
   Clap, clap, clap your hands, (*sing and do action*)
   Early in the morning. (*sing*)

2. Use other actions to involve other parts of the body. Examples are:

   Stamp your feet . . .
   Nod your head . . .
   Swing your arms . . .
   Blink your eyes . . .
   Hop around . . .
   Join your hands . . .

Variation/Way to Extend:

• Use *The Fireside Book of Children's Songs,* collected and edited by **Marie Winn (New** York: Simon & Schuster, 1966). It contains the words and music to many traditional nursery songs, singing games, and rounds.

II-9 OBSTACLE COURSE

Subject Area: Gross Motor Game

Concept/Skill: Coordinates body movements

Objectives: The children will jump, hop, crawl, skip, walk, leap, run, and gallop through an obstacle course.

Materials: • Objects such as chairs, cardboard boxes, barrels, milk cartons, ropes, ladders, and tires

Procedure:

1. Set up an obstacle course either indoors in a large open area or outdoors.
2. With your help if necessary, let the children decide what to do when they get to each object. Should they jump over it? Run around it? Crawl under it?
3. Tell the children to try to go through the course without upsetting the objects.
4. With older three-year-olds, tell them to try going through the course without touching the objects or using their hands.

Variation/Way to Extend:

• Listen to the recording *You Are Special* by Fred Rogers, published by Columbia Records (#CC24518).

Weekly Subtheme: Self-Concept

II–10 ME, MYSELF, AND I

Subject Area: Social Studies and Art

Concepts/Skills: Points to and names body parts
Develops fine motor movements of finger strength and dexterity

Objectives: The children will draw and finger-paint large images of themselves.

Materials:
- Large roll of white butcher paper
- One black crayon
- Finger paints
- Newspaper
- Scissors

Procedure:

1. Cut the roll of paper into large pieces, longer than the height of each child.
2. Spread out the newspaper on the floor.
3. Place the white sheets of paper on the newspaper.
4. Have each child lie down on his or her back on a piece of white paper while you trace around him or her with the crayon.
5. Using the tracing as an outline, encourage the child to finger-paint the outlined body.
6. As the child paints, discuss body parts. Assist with the names and functions of each.
7. When the paintings are dry, cut them out and display.

Variations/Ways to Extend:

- Begin a "Talk-About-Ourselves Time" by displaying the finger paintings of each child. With a small group, discuss how we look, parts of our bodies, and what we like about our bodies.
- Sing "Hokey Pokey" from the album *Music for Early Childhood,* published by American Book Company.

II–11 WHEELS ON THE BUS

Subject Area: Music

Concepts/Skills: Repeats a simple song
Acts out simple everyday activities
Plays using symbols

Objectives: The children will learn a new song and recall how they travel to school.

Materials:
- Pictures of buses
- Words to song

Procedure:

1. Discuss how the children in the class travel to school (by bus, by car, on foot). Invite some willing children to act out their ways of travel.

2. Tell the children that they are going to take a pretend ride on a bus with their friends. Show the picture of the buses.

3. Teach the children the following action song entitled "The Wheels on the Bus." The words and music may be found in *This Is Music for Kindergarten and Nursery School* by A. McCall (Boston: Allyn and Bacon, 1967):

    The wheels on the bus go 'round and 'round
    'Round and 'round, 'round and 'round
    The wheels on the bus go 'round and 'round
    As we ride to school.

    The lights on the bus go on and off
    On and off, on and off
    The lights on the bus go on and off
    As we ride to school.

4. Continue the song with these actions:

    Horn (beep, beep, beep) . . .
    Wipers (swish, swish, swish) . . .
    Baby (waa, waa, waa) . . .
    Mommy (shh, shh, shh) . . .
    Children (up and down, up and down, up and down) . . .
    Driver (move on back, move on back, move on back) . . .

Variations/Ways to Extend:

- Have the children role play a bus driver, people riding on the bus, and other related characters.
- Provide cardboard boxes large enough for two children to sit in and encourage dramatic play (riding on a bus, collecting tickets, the motions included in the song).

II–12 BOLOGNA AND CHEESE ANIMALS

Subject Area: Nutrition and Foods Experience

Concepts/Skills: Develops fine motor movement of hand–eye coordination
Feels good about self and abilities
Begins participation in a group

Objectives: The children will create animal shape sandwiches and demonstrate table routines and manners

Materials:
- Raisins
- Natural bologna (sliced)
- Unprocessed cheese (sliced)
- Juice
- Whole wheat bread (sliced)
- Animal-cookie cutters
- Paper plates
- Paper cups
- Napkins

Procedure:

1. After the children have washed their hands, give each of them a slice of bread that has been cut in half.
2. Then give each child a slice of bologna and a slice of cheese to assemble a half sandwich.
3. Set out the animal cutters and let each child cut shapes into their sandwich. They might want to add raisins for animal eyes.
4. Divide the class into small groups. Select a different group of children to set the table, distribute the juice, distribute the sandwiches, and so on.

Variations/Ways to Extend:

- Chop up any leftover bologna and cheese with a knife or in a blender. Let the children mix the mixture with a little bit of mayonnaise and spread it onto bread or crackers. This may be eaten for a snack the next day.
- Read *I Am Three* by Louise Fitzhugh (New York: Delacorte, 1982).

II–13   CLASS MURAL

Subject Area: Art

Concepts/Skills: Holds crayon with fingers
Paints with a large brush
Explores materials

Objective: The children will create a class mural.

Materials:
- Roll of newsprint
- Various art media (paints, crayons, chalk, pencils, charcoal, markers)

Procedure:

1. Spread out a roll of newsprint on the floor.
2. Divide the paper into sections by drawing a light pencil line every 12 inches or so. Each child can work within a defined area to minimize management problems. Only a small group of children should work on this at any one time.
3. Have each child add to the group mural by choosing the media with which he or she prefers to work.

Variations/Ways to Extend:

- Stress the idea of friendship by making a "hand in hand" border around the paper. Help the children trace one another's hands.
- Read *Best Friends for Frances* by Russell Hoban (New York: Harper and Row, 1969).
- Listen to "A Friend for All Seasons" on the Sesame Street album *In Harmony,* published by Warner Brothers Records.

Weekly Subtheme: Friends and School

II–14 PAPER BAG MASKS

Subject Areas: Social Studies and Art

Concepts/Skills: Understands sentences and questions as indicated by a relevant response
Understands that people are alike and different in how they look and feel

Objectives: The children will construct paper bag masks and demonstrate some emotions.

Materials:
- One large paper bag for each child
- Scissors
- Crayons
- Transparent tape
- Glue
- Paper strips or yarn
- Small paper cups

Procedure:

1. Develop a "feelings" discussion before the construction of the masks. "How can you tell if a person is happy?" "How do you act when you are happy?" "How can you tell when a friend is sad?" "Was there a time when you felt scared?" "What makes you mad?"
2. Prepare the bags ahead of time by cutting out the eye holes.
3. Have the children use crayons to draw a face representing a particular emotion. Each child may choose his or her own emotion to illustrate.

4. Use small paper cups for noses and paper strips or yarn for hair. Glue these into place.
5. Ask the children to take turns putting on their masks and displaying the particular emotion. Simply accept what the children say and acknowledge how they feel when they are expressing their emotions. You may help them clarify and think of better ways to express some of those feelings. For example, if a child says that sometimes he or she gets so mad that he or she feels like hitting, you can accept this and then add, "How else can we let someone know that we feel angry? Yes, we can tell that person, and tell that person why we are angry so that he or she won't do it again."

Variations/Ways to Extend:

- Using the masks and their own words, allow the children to act out their emotions with one another.
- Read *A Friend Is Someone Who Likes You* by Joan W. Anglund (San Diego, CA: Harcourt Brace Jovanovich, 1958).

II–15 OUR SPECIAL TREE

Subject Area: Science

Concepts/Skills: Observes objects closely
Understands that seeds grow into plants and trees

Objectives: The children will observe and describe a tree and recognize the passing of the seasons.

Material: • An outdoor deciduous tree

Procedure:

1. As a group, decide on a nearby tree to be your special tree for the year. As the seasons pass, visit the tree and notice the changes that occur.
2. Ask the children to help take care of the tree and any of its inhabitants. The children might hang birdfeeders from the branches for winter birds. **(Important: These birdfeeders must be maintained, as the birds will come to rely on them as a food source in the winter.)**
3. Ask a variety of questions about your tree and let the children discover the answers.
   • Gather leaves from the tree and invite each child to examine them. Ask about their colors and shapes. Why are some leaves from the same tree larger than others? Compare these leaves with leaves from another tree.
   • What kinds of seeds can you find from this tree? Is it a fruit tree? Are there acorns?
   • Is this the tallest or smallest tree around?
   • What about the bark? Touch it. Is it smooth or rough? What color is it? Make some rubbings on thick, flexible paper using crayons.
   • Does the tree have dirt or flowers around it? Do the roots show?
   • Can we find any insects on the tree? Any ants or caterpillars?
   • What else lives in our tree, any squirrels or chipmunks?
4. Find out about nesting materials used by the birds in your area. Perhaps your children will want to provide some of these to encourage and help the birds to nest in your special tree.

Variations/Ways to Extend:

• As a class project, help the children to draw their tree on a large sheet of paper, keeping the branches bare. Ask them to tear green leaves from paper and tape these onto the tree. In time, replace these with red, orange, and yellow leaves, and then brown. Remove all the leaves as winter arrives. The children can then use tiny white pieces of paper on the branches and pretend that they are snowflakes. In spring, the children can begin the process again with little green leaves.
• Take a photograph of the tree each time it is visited by the children. The photos can be used in a book along with sentences dictated by the children to you about their visits.

HARVEST TIME AND THE FARM

- ○ Colors
- ○ Foods
- ○ Farm and Farm Animals
- ○ Halloween

II–16   PRESERVED AUTUMN LEAVES

Subject Area: Math

Concepts/Skills: Observes objects closely
Sorts objects into two given categories

Objective: The children will apply a method of leaf preservation.

Materials:
- Autumn leaves with stems
- Pan
- Heat source
- Two to three inches of water
- Newspaper
- Paraffin

Procedure:

1. Put the water into the pan and heat it on a stove or other heat source. (**Caution:** Be sure the children stay away from the heat.)
2. Drop in the paraffin. When it has melted, remove the pan from the heat source.
3. Taking every precaution, let each child dip the leaves into the pan to coat the leaves with wax.
4. Dry the waxed leaves on newspaper.
5. Have the children note that the leaves will still gradually change color but will not wrinkle and dry up.
6. Have the children classify the leaves by two categories, such as size and color, or shape and color.
7. Discuss in simple terms the reasons why leaves change color. (The green color comes from chlorophyll, which turns sunlight, water, minerals, and air into food to help trees grow. When this work ends, the leaves fall and the trees rest all winter long. When the green chlorophyll goes out of the leaves, other colors (red, yellow, orange) that are always in the leaves under the green begin to show.)

Variation/Way to Extend:

- Read *The Mixed-Up Chameleon* by Eric Carle (New York: Harper and Row, 1975).

II–17   LEAVES OF COLOR

Subject Area: Creative Dramatics/Movement

Concepts/Skills: Develops creative movements
Matches colors
Repeats a simple four-line rhyme

Objectives: The children will recall the words to a rhyme about colored leaves and express themselves through body movement.

Materials:
- Two paper leaf shapes of each color: red, yellow, orange, and brown
- Safety pins
- Words to the rhyme
- Background music

Procedure:

1. For background music, play Haydn's "Autumn Leaves" from the *Surprise Symphony.*
2. Pin a colored leaf onto each child.
3. Have the children learn the words and demonstrate the actions to following rhyme:

   Twirling, twirling, twirling around,
       Softly falling to the ground.
   Red and yellow, orange and brown,
       Fall the autumn leaves.

4. Ask each child to find the child wearing the same color leaf and dance with that partner to the music.

Variations/Ways to Extend:

- Call out pairs of children by color to dance. For example, "Will the yellow leaves come up and dance?"
- Read the Caldecott Honors book *Mr. Rabbit and the Lovely Present* by Charlotte Zolotow (New York: Harper and Row, 1962).

II–18 FALL IS HERE

Subject Area: Science

Concepts/Skills: Names concrete objects in environment
Observes and explores

Objective: The children will analyze objects related to fall.

Materials:
- Table
- Small boxes
- Insect houses
- Pumpkins, apples, leaves, acorns, pine cones, Indian corn, chrysanthemums, dried weeds, corn husks
- Magnifying glasses
- Pictures and big-picture resource books of fall

Procedure:

1. Set up a table where you and the children can put items brought in that tell autumn is here. Also have small boxes, an insect house, magnifying glasses, pictures of fall, and big-picture resource books on the table.
2. Help the children identify the objects they have brought in and discover their outstanding characteristics, such as color, shape, size, weight, texture, name, and use. If it is an insect, add habits, what it eats, what it does, how it moves, what sounds it makes, and safety precautions.
Note: *Fall is Here!* by Dorothy Sterling (New York: Natural History Publications, no date) is a very good reference for teachers.

Variations/Ways to Extend:

- Using objects from your learning center, ask the children questions involving matching characteristics, such as "What color is this leaf? Yes, that's right. It is yellow. Each of you look around the room and find something else that is yellow." "What shape is this nut? That's right. It is round. Each of you look around the room and find something else that is round." You might also use sets of two cards with identical pictures of fall objects to match.
- Play "What Am I?" after discussing autumn. "I am tall and green and have needles. What am I?" "I have gray fur and like to eat nuts. What am I?" "I am big and round and orange. What am I?"

II-19 ROLY-POLY CATERPILLAR

Subject Areas: Language Arts and Art

Concepts/Skills: Repeats a simple fingerplay
Paints with a large brush
Pastes

Objective: The children will construct egg-carton caterpillars.

Materials:
- One egg carton for every two children
- Paints
- Large paintbrushes
- Pipe cleaners
- Glue
- Cotton balls
- Dry powdered paint
- Words to fingerplay

Procedure:

1. Remove the lid from an egg carton and cut the bottom portion in half lengthwise to make two caterpillars.
2. Let the children paint their caterpillars in any colors they choose.
3. Use the pipe cleaners as antennae (feelers). Glue these into place.
4. Help the children dip cotton balls in dry powdered paint and glue them onto the humps to make the caterpillar fuzzy.
5. After the caterpillars are complete, teach the children the following fingerplay entitled "Roly-Poly Caterpillar":

   Roly-poly caterpillar (*walk finger across left palm*)
   Into a corner crept, (*fold up fingers of left hand*)
   Spun around itself a blanket, (*make winding motion around hand*)
   Then for a long time slept. (*pretend to sleep; close eyes*)
   Roly-poly caterpillar
   Wakening by and by (*pretend to wake; open eyes*)
   Found itself with beautiful wings, (*put thumbs together; flutter fingers like wings*)
   Changed to a butterfly. (*fly the butterfly away*)

Variations/Ways to Extend:

- Have the children make butterflies out of construction paper and a clothespin. Let each child choose a sheet of colored construction paper that has been cut into the shape of a butterfly. Tell the children they can paint these or color them with markers, and then slip them between clothespin prongs and glue in place.

II–20   FALL MURAL

Subject Area: Art

Concepts/Skills: Creatively expresses self
Develops fine motor movements of pasting and holding crayons with fingers
Understands prepositions and prepositional phrases

Objective: The children will create a fall mural using preserved leaves.

Materials: • Leaves from activity II–16, "Preserved Autumn Leaves"
• Kraft paper
• Sponges in small pieces
• Brown crayons
• Glue
• Newspaper
• Blue, gray, and green paints

Procedure:

1. After the children have completed activity II–16, have them work on a fall mural. Prepare a large work space on the floor by first covering it with newspaper.
2. Lay the kraft paper (sized to cover your chosen wall space) on top of the newspaper.
3. Let a few children sponge-paint a sky by using blues and grays on the top half of the paper.
4. Ask a few other children to sponge-paint green grass on the bottom half of the paper.
5. When dry, have the children draw in tree trunks by holding their unwrapped brown crayons sideways and using bold strokes to make tree trunks and branches.
6. Help the children glue their preserved autumn leaves onto the branches. Talk about placing leaves *under, on, off, on top of,* or *on the bottom of* the tree.
7. When the mural is complete, hang it on the chosen wall space at the children's eye level.

Variations/Ways to Extend:

• Instead of the preserved leaves, you might have the children make their own leaves by tearing them out of red, orange, and yellow tissue paper.
• Help the children dip each hand, palm side down, into separate containers of fall-colored paints. They can then press their hands onto the tree trunks in different positions to create a leaf effect. After washing their hands after each color, the children can choose other colors to use.
• Read *Down Come the Leaves* by Henrietta Bancroft (New York: Harper and Row, 1961).

II-21 HOMEMADE APPLESAUCE

Subject Area: Nutrition and Foods Experience

Concepts/Skills: Shows curiosity and the need to explore anything new
Measures
Follows directions

Objectives: The children will observe how to and help make applesauce.

Materials:
- Measuring cup
- Knife
- Wooden spoon
- Stove or other heat source
- Pot with a cover
- Potholder
- Four apples
- ⅓ cup water
- ¼ cup honey
- Lemon juice
- Raisins

Procedure:

1. Wash, peel, core, and cut each apple into quarters.
2. Put the apples and water into a pot and set on a stove or other heat source over low heat. **(Caution:** Be sure the children stay away from the knife and the heat source.)
3. Cover the pot and gently cook the apples about fifteen minutes or until soft. Stir occasionally.
4. Add the honey and a little lemon juice and stir until the mixture is well blended.
5. Remove the pot from the heat and mash the apples until either smooth or slightly chunky. Add a few raisins.
6. Serve the applesauce warm or chilled.

Variations/Ways to Extend:

- For a special applesauce treat, stir in ½ cup crushed pineapple, chopped walnuts, and a dash of cinnamon. Chill for four hours.
- Obtain an 11″ × 14″ art reproduction of "Still Life: Apples on Pink Tablecloth" (#1833) by Henri Matisse from the National Gallery of Art, Publications Service, Washington, D.C. 20565. Be sure to write for a catalog and prices.

Weekly Subtheme: Foods

II-22 TO MARKET, TO MARKET

Subject Area: Social Studies

Concepts/Skills: Shows curiosity and the need to investigate anything new
Names plural form to refer to more than one
Enjoys being with other children

Objectives: The children will visit a supermarket, observe various foods, and discuss them.

Material: • Supermarket

Procedure:

1. Arrange for a trip to a local supermarket. Tell the children that they are going mainly to be looking at fruits and vegetables.
2. Tour the entire store first and then arrive in the produce section. Point out the colors, shapes, and names of the various fruits and vegetables.
3. Stress the idea of singular versus plural forms; for example, one orange in a display of many oranges. Ask the children to repeat the plural form for several of the fruits and vegetables seen.
4. Use this opportunity to also have the children use their sense of smell and to engage them in some counting and weighing activities. You might also hold up some frozen or canned goods to enable the children to compare these forms with those in the fresh food section.
5. Buy each child a fresh carrot, apple, or banana, and thank the store's manager for his or her cooperation.

Variation/Way to Extend:

• Set up a supermarket in the classroom. Ask the children to bring empty boxes and containers from home.

II-23   ALL ABOUT FOOD

Subject Area: Thinking Games

Concepts/Skills: Places objects on their outlines
Recognizes which item doesn't belong
Identifies what is missing
Recalls two or more objects visually presented

Objective: The children will participate in several games related to foods.

Materials: • Pictures of different types of foods
• Variety of real foods

Procedure:

1. Play "Food Lotto." Make a food shape chart with matching cards. Ask the children to place the proper cards on the outlines.
2. Play "What Doesn't Belong?" Display four pictures. Ask such questions as "Which is not a food?" "Which is not a fruit?" "Which is canned?"
3. Play "What Is Missing?" Have four pictures of foods or four real foods and ask the children to cover their eyes while you take one item away. Ask the children to say which item is missing.
4. Play "Sequence Patterning." Arrange a sequence of two, three, four, or more food pictures and have the children take turns reproducing the same sequence.
5. Play "Picture Memory." Hold up a picture of a food for a few seconds and then put it down. Ask the children to tell something about the picture they just saw.

Variations/Ways to Extend:

• Encourage a sensory experience with foods. Have the children see, hear, touch, smell, and taste the many qualities of foods. You might also have the children compare, contrast, and describe a variety of foods.
• Read *Walter the Baker* by Eric Carle (New York: Alfred A. Knopf, 1972).

II-24 SPONGE PAINTING

Subject Area: Art

Concepts/Skills: Holds a brush and sponge
Paints

Objective: The children will create paintings of apple orchards or pumpkin patches.

Materials:
- Paintbrushes
- Paper
- Clip clothespins
- Red, orange, green, and brown paints
- Sponges cut in large ovals and in small circles
- Pictures of apple orchards and pumpkin patches

Procedure:

1. Display pictures of and discuss apple orchards and pumpkin patches. If possible, arrange a visit to either of these places.
2. Ask the children to choose which of these places they would like to paint.
3. Have the children use green and brown paints for vines and tree trunks.
4. Attach a clip clothespin to each sponge piece. Then have the children dab a sponge oval into the orange paint to create a "pumpkin patch" or a sponge circle into the red paint to create an "apple orchard."

Variation/Way to Extend:

- Teach the children this fingerplay entitled "The Apple Tree."

    Way up in the apple tree (*point up*)
    Two red apples smiled at me. (*close thumb and forefinger*)
    I shook the tree as hard as I could. (*grab imaginary tree and shake*)
    Down fell the apples, (*hold hands and arms high, then let them fall*)
    M-m-m, they were good! (*rub tummy and smile*)

II-25 FRUIT FUN

Subject Area: Science

Concept/Skill: Demonstrates accurate sense of taste, touch, sight, and smell

Objectives: The children will identify several fruits and their method of growth and will make and eat fruit kabobs.

Materials:
- Peaches, bananas, strawberries, and other fruits
- Water
- Knife
- Toothpicks
- Colander
- Pictures of fruit growing on trees, bushes, vines, and plants

Procedure:

1. Discuss where fruits grow: trees (apples, peaches, oranges); bushes (blueberries, gooseberries); vines (strawberries, melons, pumpkins); and plants (bananas, pineapples).
2. Ask the children, "How does the fruit get to us?" Help them realize that the process includes farmers, pickers, packers, refrigerator trucks, ships, trains, and planes. Say, "Fruit is good to eat just as nature grows it. What other ways can we try fruit?" (canned, frozen, dried)
3. Discuss size, shape, color, texture, and ripeness of fruits. Wash and prepare pieces of fruit for fruit kabobs. Skewer the pieces on toothpicks and serve as a snack.

Variations/Ways to Extend:

- Many field trip possibilities emerge with this area of study. You might consider an apple or cherry orchard, cider factory, outdoor market, neighbor's garden, pumpkin patch, or botanical gardens.
- Read the Caldecott Honor Book *Blueberries for Sal* by Robert McCloskey (New York: Viking, 1948).

II-26 FARM ANIMAL MATCH

Subject Area: Social Studies

Concepts/Skills: Pairs related pictures
Understands that there are many kinds of animals

Objectives: The children will identify farm animals from cards, classify them, and demonstrate their behaviors.

Material: • Sets of cards (can be made from stickers or gummed seals)

Procedure:

1. Have the children hold adult animal cards and try to match the adult animal with its baby. Example: horse, colt.
2. Have the children hold adult animal cards and try to match the animal with the food product it gives us. Example: chicken, egg.
3. Deal the cards and ask each child to imitate the sounds of the animals he or she is holding. The other children must try to guess the animals. Example: cow, *moo*.

Variation/Way to Extend:

• Teach the children this fingerplay entitled "Ten Little Ponies."

Ten little ponies (*hold up ten fingers*)
Go for a gallop; (*move hands to the right*)
They go for a trot; (*move hands to the left*)
They come to a halt
In the big feed lot. (*keep hands still*)
Ten little ponies
Fat and well fed, (*pat stomach*)
Curl up together (*curl fingers*)
In a soft straw bed. (*lay fingers in lap*)

II–27 ALL ABOUT FARMS

Subject Area: Science

Concepts/Skills: Understands that there are many kinds of animals
Listens to stories
Puts together a six- to seven-piece puzzle

Objective: The children will make observations about the farm from several books, pictures, and a discussion.

Materials:
- *Animals on a Farm* by Feodor Rojankovsky (New York: Alfred A. Knopf, 1967)
- *Big Red Barn* by Margaret W. Brown (Reading, MA: Addison-Wesley, 1956)
- *The Little Farm* by Lois Lenski (New York: McKay, 1942)
- Judy puzzles
- Pictures of farm animals

Procedure:

1. Ask the children what a farm is (a piece of land, usually large, used to raise crops or animals; it is usually located outside a city or town).
2. Try to arrange a visit to a farm in your area.
3. Read one of the books listed here. Then show pictures of chickens, ducks, cows, pigs, horses, turkeys, sheep, and other animals.
4. Explain how farm animals help the farmer:

   Horses provide transportation and pull wagons
   Chickens lay eggs
   Cows and goats give milk
   Cats catch mice
   Dogs guard other animals
   Sheep supply wool
   Bees make honey

5. Have the children work with Judy puzzles of farm animals, such as the seven-piece puzzle "Horse and Foal." These puzzles are available from the Judy Co., Judy Instructional Materials, 250 James Street, Morristown, NJ 07966. Be sure to write for a catalog and prices.

Variations/Ways to Extend:
- Teach the children the song "Old MacDonald Had a Farm."
- Prepare cards to help the children recall the sequence of certain procedures performed on a farm. Limit these to three events, such as chickens are fed and tended; chickens lay eggs; and eggs are collected.
- Obtain an 11″ × 14″ art reproduction of "The Cornell Farm" (#1936) by Edward Hicks from the National Gallery of Art, Publications Service, Washington, DC 20565. Be sure to write for a catalog and prices.

II-28 WHAT CAN WE DO WITH MILK?

Subject Area: Nutrition and Foods Experience

Concepts/Skills: Demonstrates accurate sense of smell and taste
Understands relationship of items within a category

Objectives: The children will identify and compare four milk products.

Materials:
- Milk
- Several varieties of cheese
- Ice cream
- Yogurt
- Toothpicks
- Spoons
- Small bowls
- Napkins

Procedure:

1. Prior to this activity, discuss where milk comes from. Limit the discussion to the fact that milk comes from cows, farmers milk the cows, and a refrigerated truck takes the milk from the farm to the dairy plant, where it is put into containers.
2. Let the children see, smell, and feel the containers of milk and milk products.
3. Discuss their colors and aromas.
4. Encourage the children to tell about their favorite dairy foods.
5. Cut the cheeses into cubes and place onto toothpicks so that everyone can taste them. Discuss how they look and taste different.
6. Let the children taste and compare the ice cream and yogurt.
7. Ask the children, "Why do we drink milk and eat dairy products?" Tell them about healthy bones, teeth, and skin.

Variations/Ways to Extend:

- Let the children help make a yogurt shake for snack time. Point out the dairy products in the following recipe as you put each ingredient into a blender:

  1 cup plain yogurt
  1 cup ice cream
  ½ cup milk
  ½ cup fruit (such as strawberries)
  1 tablespoon jam (such as strawberry jam)

- Recite the poem "The Cow" by Robert Louis Stevenson.

THE COW
The friendly cow all red and white,
　I love with all my heart:
She gives me cream with all her might,
　To eat with apple tart.

She wanders lowing here and there,
　And yet she cannot stray,
All in the pleasant open air,
　The pleasant light of day;

And blown by all the winds that pass
　And wet with all the showers,
She walks among the meadow grass
　And eats the meadow flowers.

II-29 UNDER THE FLAP

Subject Area: Math

Concepts/Skills: Understands number concepts
Counts the number of objects in a set

Objectives: The children will count pictures of chicks and identify the corresponding numeral.

Materials:
- Two sheets of posterboard
- Scissors
- Tape
- Markers

Procedure:

1. Cut five flaps on a large sheet of posterboard, in any arrangement. Tape this sheet to another sheet of posterboard of the same size.
2. Draw sets of chicks (or use animal stickers) from one to five on top of each flap. Under the flap (on the back sheet) write the corresponding numeral.
3. Have the children count the number of chicks on the flap. If they count correctly, let them lift the flap and see the corresponding numeral.
4. Discuss how the numeral represents that number of objects.

Variation/Way to Extend:

- Discuss the idea that a "set" is a group of things that are alike or that "go together" in the same way. Have identical cards of the chicks for the children to match to those on the posterboard flaps.

II–30   THE FARMER IN THE DELL

Subject Area: Music and Creative Dramatics

Concepts/Skills: Memorizes and repeats a simple song
Dramatizes a simple story

Objective: The children will dramatize a song.

Materials: • Props for the song's characters (farmer—straw hat, kerchief; wife—bonnet, apron; animals—paper ears and tails attached to headbands)

Procedure:

1. First teach the children the words:

   The farmer in the dell, the farmer in the dell,
   Heigh-ho, the derry-o, the farmer in the dell.
   The farmer takes a wife . . .
   The wife takes a child . . .
   The child takes a nurse . . .
   The nurse takes a dog . . .
   The dog takes a cat . . .
   The cat takes a rat . . .
   The rat takes the cheese . . .
   The cheese stands alone . . .

2. Then have the children form a circle with one child acting as the "farmer" and standing in the center of the circle.

3. Ask the children to join hands and sing the words while moving around the farmer. Then that farmer chooses a wife, who stands in the center also. Then the wife chooses a child, who also stands in the center, and so on.

4. On the last verse, the child who is the cheese stands alone in the circle and can become the farmer for the next game.

Variations/Ways to Extend:

• Set up a dramatic play center with clothes for farmers (straw hats, red scarves, plaid shirts, overalls), toy barns, wagons, plastic animals, and so on. Remind the children that farmers are not always men. To encourage the children's creative impulses, supply them with only boxes, blocks, and wood scraps and let them use their imaginations to transform these objects into barnyards and animals.

• Read *Country Noisy Book* by Margaret Wise Brown (New York: Harper and Row, 1940). Be sure to emphasize the farm noises.

II-31 BIG AND ROUND PUMPKINS

Subject Area: Language Arts

Concepts/Skills: Memorizes and repeats a simple fingerplay
Participates in a group
Moves body in response to simple teacher commands

Objective: The children will act out a Halloween fingerplay.

Materials:
- Words to the fingerplay
- Pumpkin
- Newspapers
- Knife

Procedure:

1. Show the children the pumpkin and demonstrate the carving of eyes, a nose, and a mouth.

2. When completed, ask the children to stand and teach them the following fingerplay:

We are pumpkins big and round, big and round, big and round;	(*clasp hands and stretch arms out away from body*)
We are pumpkins big and round, sitting on the ground.	(*sit on floor*)
See our great big shining eyes, shining eyes, shining eyes;	(*create an oval with thumb and index finger of each hand and place over eyes*)
See our great big shining eyes, looking all around.	(*scan*)
See our great big laughing mouths, laughing mouths, laughing mouths;	(*point to mouth*)
See our great big laughing mouths, smiling right at you.	(*smile*)

Variation/Way to Extend:

- Lay down plenty of newspaper and cut into the top of the pumpkin and pull off the top and stem. Allow the children to assist in reaching into the pumpkin to remove the seeds and pulp. Save the seeds for activity II-32.

Weekly Subtheme: Halloween

II–32 ROASTED PUMPKIN SEEDS

Subject Area: Math and Science

Concepts/Skills: Understands concepts of "full" and "empty"
Develops fine motor movements of measuring and pouring

Objectives: The children will help measure and prepare seeds for roasting.

Materials:
- Two cups washed and dried pumpkin seeds from activity II–31 (paper towel dry or dry overnight for extra crispness)
- Two tablespoons melted butter
- ½ teaspoon Worcestershire sauce
- Salt
- Cookie sheet with a lip
- Wooden spoon
- Oven

Procedure:

1. Mix the dried seeds with the butter and Worcestershire sauce.
2. Spread the seeds onto the cookie sheet and sprinkle lightly with salt.
3. Bake one hour at 250° F, stirring occasionally. (**Caution:** Be sure the children stay away from the oven.) The seeds are done when they are crisp and brown.
4. Enjoy the seeds as a snack. Make sure the children chew the seeds.

Variations/Ways to Extend:

- Play "Pin the Nose (or Hat, Mouth, etc.) on the Jack-o'-Lantern." Cut out a large poster-board pumpkin and tack up with most of the features drawn in. Blindfold the children and have them try to put pre-cut features in place. (Note: Use a Halloween mask with eye holes blocked out instead of a blindfold. It is much quicker, easier, and more comfortable than tying a scarf around each child's head.)
- Let the children make seed collages from leftover unbaked pumpkin seeds.

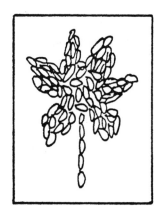

Weekly Subtheme: Halloween

II–33 PUMPKIN PERSON

Subject Area: Art

Concepts/Skills: Develops fine motor movement of pasting

Learns parts of a face

Objective: The children will construct paper pumpkin people.

Materials:
- 9″ × 12″ sheets of orange construction paper
- Facial parts cut from black construction paper
- Strips of orange paper pre-folded accordion-style
- Scissors
- Pencils
- Paste
- String

Procedure:

1. Assist each child in folding a 9″ × 12″ sheet of orange paper in half.
2. Let the child draw half of a big pumpkin shape on one half and, using the fold as the center of the pumpkin, help the child cut out the shape.
3. Unfold the paper and have the child paste on facial features made from black construction paper.
4. Distribute the folded strips of orange paper. These will be used as springs for **arms and legs.**
5. Have the children cut out hands and feet from black paper and paste them to the ends of the springs.
6. Help the children paste the arms and legs to the pumpkin faces.
7. Hang the pumpkin people by string from the ceiling.

Variations/Ways to Extend:

- Paste pumpkin seeds onto the pumpkin head as facial features.
- Make these pumpkin people into masks by cutting out the facial features and letting the children glue tongue depressors to the bottom of each mask (for holding).

II–34   PUMPKIN MUFFINS

Subject Area: Nutrition

Concepts/Skills: Develops fine motor movements of measuring, pouring, and mixing
Demonstrates accurate sense of touch, smell, and taste

Objectives: The children will observe and participate in baking pumpkin muffins.

Materials: (This recipe makes twelve muffins)
- 1 egg
- ½ cup milk
- ½ cup canned pumpkin
- ¼ cup melted margarine
- 1½ cups whole wheat flour
- ½ teaspoon nutmeg
- ½ cup raisins
- Bowls
- Oven
- Potholders
- Fork
- Wooden spoon
- Muffin tins (paper baking cups are optional)
- Napkins

Procedure:

1. Let the children help with the measuring, pouring, and mixing of ingredients.
2. Beat the egg slightly with a fork. Stir in the milk, pumpkin, and margarine. Blend the dry ingredients in another bowl and then stir into the egg mixture just until the flour is moistened. The batter should be lumpy. Fold in the raisins. Fill greased muffin cups or paper baking cups ⅔ full. Sprinkle ¼ teaspoon sugar over each muffin.
3. Bake at 400° F for eighteen to twenty minutes. (**Caution:** Be sure the children stay away from the heat.)
4. Serve the muffins warm with glasses of milk or juice at snack time.

Variation/Way to Extend:

- Read *The Terrible Trick or Treat* by Edith Battles (Reading, MA: Addison-Wesley, 1970). You might want to read this book while the children are enjoying their pumpkin muffins.

II-35 HAPPY HALLOWEEN

Subject Area: Music

Concepts/Skills: Repeats a simple song
Participates with enthusiasm

Objective: The children will learn a new song about the many characters visible on Halloween.

Material: • Words and music to the song (See next page.)

Procedure:

1. Sing "Happy Halloween" to the children. Ask them to listen and hear about many kinds of costumes that they might see on Halloween.
2. Teach the chorus to the children and have them repeat it between the verses.

Variation/Way to Extend:

• Set up a costume shop. Collect fabrics and accessories that can be made into the costumes mentioned in the song as well as other costumes, such as those for a scarecrow, pirate, or ballerina.

Happy Halloween

Words and Music by **BOB MESSANO**
Arranged by John Sheehan

1. There's a ghost out-side with a jel-ly bean and a big black cat whose eyes are green C' - mon dress up let's make the scene on a Hap - py Hal - lo - ween!

Copyright 1984 by Bob Messano

Chorus: When the scaries and the spookies come out
And all the children shout!
Trick or Treat! It's fun to meet—
your friends on Halloween!

2. There's a princess talkin' to a clown
And witches runnin' all around!
Oh, can you hear the scary sounds—
On a Happy Halloween!

   (chorus)

3. When the goblins prance and the devils dance
And you can wear your daddy's pants
C'mon now let's take a chance—
On a Happy Halloween!

   (chorus)

4. When the pumpkin glows and the night wind blows
Ooooooooo!
When the pumpkin glows and the night wind blows
Ooooooooo!

   (chorus)

HOME
AND FAMILY

○ My Family

○ My Home and Neighborhood

○ American Indians

○ Thanksgiving

II-36 WHO'S IN MY FAMILY?

Subject Area: Art

Concepts/Skills: Understands that parental figures care for home and family
Draws a face with facial parts and stick arms and legs
Holds a crayon with fingers

Objective: The children will demonstrate knowledge of their families by drawing pictures of family members.

Materials: • Pictures of different types of families
• Paper
• Crayons

Procedure:

1. Show the children pictures of different types of families (single-parent, multi-racial, blended such as with stepchildren, and extended).
2. Elicit the children's thoughts about the following ideas: parental figures care for each family member; families work and play together; and families change.
3. Ask each child to draw and color a picture of his or her family, including pets. Label each family member for the child.
4. Encourage the children to dictate stories about their families as you record their words at the bottom of the picture.

Variations/Ways to Extend:

• Read *Ask Mr. Bear* by Majorie Flack (New York: Macmillan, 1971).
• The week before this activity, send notes home requesting some family (non-heirloom!) photos. Then display these photos on a bulletin board.

II-37 BABY VISIT

Subject Area: Science

Concepts/Skills: Speaks in four- to six-word sentences
Asks questions
Recognizes and names articles of clothing worn

Objectives: The children will observe an infant and ask questions about the baby.

Materials:
- *I Want to Tell You About My Baby* by Roslyn Banish (Berkeley, CA: Wingbow, 1982)
- Visitors

Procedure:

1. Read the book mentioned here as a stimulus for discussion and questions.
2. Arrange for a parent and his or her baby to visit the classroom.
3. Have the children observe the baby's facial features, feet, and hands. Discuss how the baby communicates, what foods or liquids he or she takes, and what he or she wears.
4. Encourage questions from the children.

Variations/Ways to Extend:

- Read *Nobody Asked Me If I Wanted a Baby Sister* by Martha Alexander (New York: Dial, 1971).
- As background music this week, play a recording of Brahms' lullaby "Cradle Song."

II-38 FINGER PEOPLE

Subject Area: Language Arts

Concepts/Skills: Repeats a fingerplay

Understands number concepts up to five

Objective: The children will demonstrate a fingerplay about a family.

Material: • Words to the fingerplay

Procedure:

1. Hold up one hand as you demonstrate this fingerplay to the children.

Finger people
　Are such fun
We will meet them
　One by one.
First comes mother (*wiggle index finger*)
　Next comes father (*wiggle middle finger*)
There there is
　The big brother. (*wiggle ring finger*)
Here is sister
　With her ball (*wiggle little finger*)
Here is baby
　Last of all. (*wiggle thumb*)
Now we'll count them
　Just to see
How many in our family. (*count 1, 2, 3, 4, 5*)

2. Repeat this fingerplay several times with the children.

Variations/Ways to Extend:

- Read *Families Live Together* by Esther Meeks and Elizabeth Bagwell (Chicago: Follett, no date).
- Obtain an 11″ × 14″ art reproduction of "The Copley Family" (#1650) by John Singleton Copley from the National Gallery of Art, Publications Service, Washington, DC 20565. Be sure to ask for a catalog and prices.

II-39   MOMMY'S AND DADDY'S

Subject Area: Thinking Games

Concepts/Skills: Observes objects closely
Names concrete objects in environment
Understands sentences and questions as indicated by relevant response

Objective: The children will discuss the many facets of their parents' lives by observing belongings of one another's parents.

Materials: • Objects from home belonging to parents
• Table

Procedure:

1. A week before this activity, send notes home asking for each child to bring in something that belongs to his or her father or mother.
2. Set up a special display table for these objects.
3. Have each child take a turn holding up the object he or she brought. With your guidance, ask the other children to guess facts about the object. Why was it chosen? Does it tell what kind of work the parent does? Is it something the parent and child use together? Is it something to wear? Is it something with which to decorate?
4. Use the information generated to discuss the many tasks parents perform at home and at work. Talk about the various jobs parents have, and also about what the children like most about their parents.

Variations/Ways to Extend:

• Read *The Growing Story* by Ruth Krauss (New York: Harper and Row, 1947).
• Have the children work with the Judy puzzles of family members, such as the six-piece "Helping Mother." These puzzles are available from The Judy Co., Judy Instructional Materials, 250 James Street, Morristown, NJ 07966. Be sure to write for a catalog and prices.

Weekly Subtheme: My Family

II–40 GRANDPARENTS' DAY

Subject Area: Social Studies

Concepts/Skills: Understands idea of extended family
Engages in simple conversation
Begins to understand that self and others change

Objectives: The children will observe several grandparents and contrast being young with being older.

Materials:
- Visitors
- Pencil
- Index cards

Procedure:

1. Invite some grandparents for a visit. Encourage them to bring interesting objects or photographs of themselves as children or of their childhood homes, and to tell of interesting experiences or help with some activity in the room.

2. On index cards, write questions you might ask the grandparents. Examples are:
   "Why do you like to play with your grandchildren?"
   "What is your favorite song?" (Or food, and so on.)
   "Do you have a favorite story you'd like to tell us?"
   "Do you have a hobby or something to share with us?"

Variation/Way to Extend:

- Read *Grandfather and I* (New York: Lothrop, 1959) and *Grandmother and I* (New York: Lothrop, 1961), both by Helen E. Buckley.

II–41 WHERE I LIVE

Subject Area: Art

Concepts/Skills: Paints with a large brush on paper
Pastes
Recognizes and names pieces of furniture

Objectives: The children will create paintings of their homes and have them labeled with their addresses.

Materials:
• Pre-cut family figures
• Pre-cut catalog pictures of furniture
• Newsprint
• Paste
• Brushes
• Markers
• Children's addresses
• Paints

Procedure:

1. Outline a house shape for each child on newsprint using a black marker.

2. Ask each child to paint the house in whatever color he or she wants.
3. When the paint is dry, write the child's name and address on the paper below the house.
4. Give each child pre-cut shapes of family figures that represent his or her household makeup. Have the children paste these onto their houses.
5. Give the children an assortment of simple catalog pictures of furniture and have them paste these onto their houses as well.

Variations/Ways to Extend:

• For a lively colorful display, attach the children's houses to the wall and group them by streets or areas. Make streets of black construction paper and add paper props such as cars, trees, and "stop" signs.
• Read the Caldecott Medal book *The Little House* by Virginia L. Burton (Boston: Houghton Mifflin, 1942).

Weekly Subtheme: My Home and Neighborhood

II–42 SHAPES IN A NEIGHBORHOOD

Subject Area: Math

Concepts/Skills: Matches, points to, and labels shapes
Pastes

Objectives: The children will analyze shapes and construct a picture of a neighborhood.

Materials:
- Large pre-cut basic shapes (circle, square, triangle, and rectangle)
- Construction paper
- Paste
- Paper
- Dark-colored marker
- Small neighborhood items cut from paper shapes

Procedure:

1. Cut and display large paper basic shapes. Discuss these shapes with the children.
2. Make simple neighborhood houses, trees, etc., out of circles, squares, triangles, and rectangles and outline the basic shapes with a marker.

3. Give some of these neighborhood items to the children and ask them to first name the object (tree, sun, truck) and then match the shape it's made from to one of the large shapes on display. Ask the children to tell the name of each shape.
4. Let the children play with these shapes and use them to construct a neighborhood by arranging and pasting them on paper.

Variation/Way to Extend:

- Read *Wake Up City* by Alvin R. Tresselt (New York: Lothrop, 1956).

II–43 SOUNDS IN THE NEIGHBORHOOD

Subject Area: Language Arts

Concepts/Skills: Identifies common sounds
Names concrete objects in the environment

Objectives: The children will identify sounds and pictures of sound-producing things and make a montage.

Materials:
- Pictures of neighborhood things that make noise
- Scissors
- Paste
- Tape recorder or cassette player
- Tape of neighborhood sounds

Procedure:

1. Introduce this activity by asking the children to orally list things in their neighborhood that make noise (cars, buses, church bells, children playing, dogs barking, machinery).
2. Play the tape of recorded neighborhood sounds and see if the children can identify each one. Ask the children to then match the sounds to the pictures.
3. Have the children make a sound montage of the pictures by pasting them on paper.

Variations/Ways to Extend:

- Read *Whistle for Willie* by Ezra J. Keats (New York: Viking, 1964).
- Many varied sounds are recorded on the album *The Counting Color and Sound ABC's*. One entire side of the album is called "Sounds All Around Us" and contains a multitude of clear, common sounds. Available from Wonderland Records, Division of A.A. Records, Inc., 1105 Globe Avenue, Mountainside, NJ 07092, Dept. WR.

II–44   THIS IS THE WAY . . .

Subject Area: Music

Concepts/Skills: Memorizes and repeats a simple song
Understands that parental figures care for home and family

Objectives: The children will sing about jobs to accomplish in the home and act them out.

Materials:
- Words to the song
- Props (optional)

Procedure:

1. Sing this children's favorite with many verses describing jobs to do around the house. Encourage the children to help their parents with these activities at home.

   This is the way we wash the clothes,
     Wash the clothes, wash the clothes.
   This is the way we wash the clothes,
     So early Monday morning.
   This is the way we vacuum the floor . . .
     . . . So early Tuesday morning.
   This is the way we paint the house . . .
     . . . So early Wednesday morning.
   (*continue through the week*)

2. Have the children demonstrate the motions they are singing. Props can be used if you want.

Variations/Ways to Extend:

- Read *Beady Bear* by Don Freeman (New York: Viking, 1954).
- Discuss what jobs the children do to help at home. Use these suggestions as additional lyrics and actions in the song.

II–45 SPONGE PLANT

Subject Area: Science

Concept/Skill: Understands that seeds need water, light, and air to grow into plants

Objective: The children will construct hanging plants to help decorate their homes.

Materials:
- Sponges
- String
- Water
- Parsley seeds
- Plastic wrap
- Stapler
- Notes to parents

Procedure:

1. Staple a different piece of string to each corner of a rectangular sponge and tie together for hanging.
2. Wet the sponge and have the children sprinkle it with parsley seeds.
3. Wrap the planter in plastic for carrying home and attach a note instructing parents to remove the wrap and hang the sponge in a sunny window. Ask the parents to keep the sponges damp with water. The seeds will grow into plants and cover the sponge.

4. Discuss with the children how the seeds need water, light, and air to grow into plants.

Variation/Way to Extend:

- Look at the pictures in *Seeds and More Seeds* by Millicent Selsam (New York: Harper and Row, 1959).

II–46   DRUM BEAT

Subject Area: Music

Concepts/Skills: Participates in and appreciates music
Moves body in response to simple teacher commands
Claps along to a beat
Develops gross motor movements of walking, hopping, jumping, and running

Objective: The children will demonstrate a response to a rhythm pattern through movement.

Materials: • Small drums (Native American type if possible)

Procedure:

1. Discuss with the children the use of the drum in the Native American culture. (It is a means of communication and celebration.) Tell the children that American Indians frequently made drums by completely hollowing out a tree trunk and then stretching two tanned leather hides across the openings on either end. These were held in place with leather thongs.
2. Invite half the children to beat on the drums while the other children move creatively to the beat. Encourage a 1-2-3-4 drum beat, having the children clap the beat first, and then beat the drums. Ask the other children to walk, run, jump, and hop on one foot to the beat. They can also dance by alternating their feet with a toe-heel–toe-heel movement.
3. Have the two groups then switch activities.

Variation/Way to Extend:

• Allow the children to vary the beat and think up other ways to move. such as silently, joyfully, and stiffly.
Special Note·

Use the terms "American Indians" or "Native Americans" when teaching this and the following lessons. Be sensitive to the stereotyping of American Indians by avoiding such phrases as "Sit like an Indian" or "Hop like an Indian."

The activities found in this section attempt to introduce some of the richness of American Indian culture. Realize, however, that there are more than 200 nations, each one separate and distinct.

More information on teaching about Native Americans can be obtained by writing to:

Council on Interracial Books for Children
1841 Broadway
New York, New York 10023
(Ask for *Unlearning "Indian" Stereotypes*
and *Books for Equity*)

Mohawk Nation
Rooseveltown, New York 13683
(Ask for posters, booklists, and "Akwesasne Notes")

Instructor Publications
Danville, New York 14437
(Ask for prints, teacher guides, posters, and a catalog)

Native American Educational Program
P.S. 199
West 107th Street
New York, New York 10025
(Ask for information about posters and records)

Museum of the American Indian
Broadway at 155th Street
New York, New York 10032
(Ask for information on slides and books and a catalog)

II–47 FEATHER COUNT

Subject Area: Math

Concept/Skill: Understands number concepts

Objective: The children will count feathers.

Materials: • Six pre-cut construction paper feathers (see the pattern on next page)

Procedure:

1. Explain to the children that feathers are used by Native Americans to decorate objects and to make headdresses.
2. Sitting in front of the children, place one or more (up to six) feathers on a table or on the floor. Then ask one child at a time to count the paper feathers from left to right.
3. Continue this procedure, varying the number of shapes presented and allowing each child to participate in identifying the number of feathers.

Variations/Ways to Extend:

- Cut feather shapes from different-colored construction paper and allow the children to sort the feathers based on color. You might also cut the shapes in different sizes and have the children sort them according to large and small.
- Number each feather. Tape the feathers to the wall and allow the children to rote count them in sequence from left to right.
- Read *Indian Two Feet & His Eagle Feather* by Margaret Friskey (Chicago: Childrens Press, 1967).

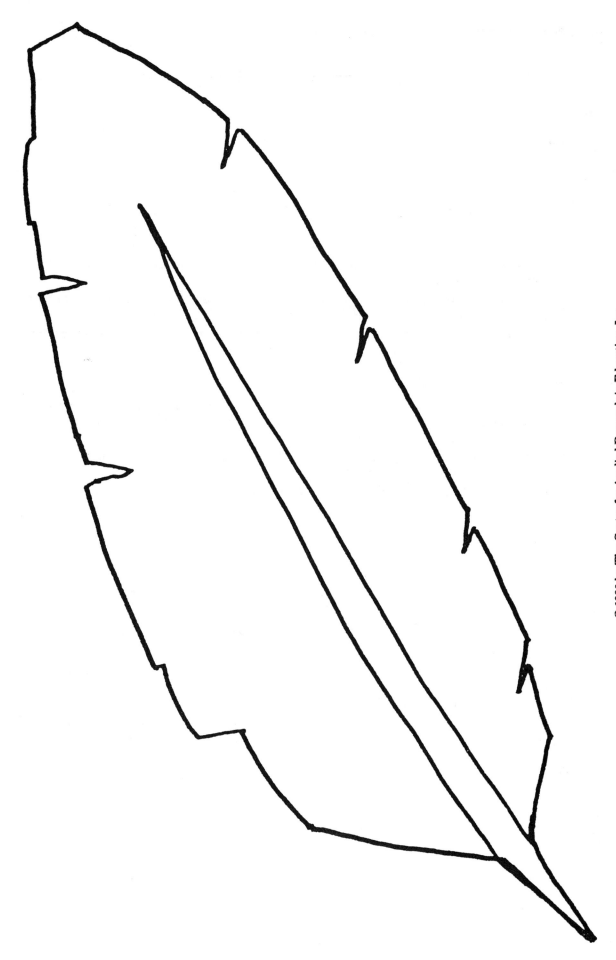

II–48 INDIAN NECKLACE

Subject Area: Art

Concepts/Skills: Strings macaroni
Points to colors on command
Recognizes a pattern

Objective: The children will construct a colorful necklace from dyed macaroni.

Materials:
- Macaroni
- Plastic cord
- Food coloring
- Paper towels

Procedure:

1. Dye the macaroni many different colors with the food coloring and allow to dry on paper towels.
2. Use the plastic cord to string the necklace as it (the cord) is stiff enough to make no needle necessary.
3. Encourage the children to follow a patterning sequence, such as yellow-red-yellow or orange-green-orange.
4. Tie a knot at the ends and let the children wear them.

Variations/Ways to Extend:
- String doughnut-shaped cereal instead of macaroni or use colored paper rectangles with holes in the center.
- Read *American Indian Music and Musical Instruments* by George S. Fichter (New York: McKay, 1978) for some good ideas on how to make gourd rattles, clappers, jingler anklets, and other items. You will have to make these instruments, but the children can decorate them and use them.

II–49 INDIAN TRAIL

Subject Area: Gross Motor Games

Concepts/Skills: Balances
Walks forward and backward
Walks on tiptoe

Objectives: The children will walk between two long pieces of string and keep their balance.

Materials: • Two pieces of eight-foot-long string
• Tape

Procedure:

1. Discuss the idea that many American Indians lived among the forests and wore out trails in the woods by traveling the same path over and over.
2. Tape two pieces of eight-foot-long string eight inches apart on the floor. Tell the children that this is an Indian trail.
3. Ask the children to walk the trail without stepping out of the lines. Tell them they can use their outstretched arms for balance and, if they want, can walk on tiptoe, quietly, as an Indian would in the forest. Also ask the children to walk backward along the trail.
4. As the children become proficient, place the strings only four inches apart.
5. Then have the children try walking (both forward and backward) directly *on* one of the strings, after you have removed the others.

Variations/Ways to Extend:

• Read *Indian Two Feet & His Horse* by Margaret Friskey (Chicago, Childrens Press, 1959).
• For background music, play "Music of the American Indian" (RCA Victor Elementary Record Library).

II-50 MAKING POPCORN

Subject Area: Nutrition and Food Experience

Concepts/Skills: Measures
Observes change in form
Begins something and enjoys the finished product

Objective: The children will observe the popping of corn kernels into popcorn.

Materials:
- Popcorn
- Oil
- Butter
- Salt
- Large bowl
- Measuring cup
- Napkins
- Popcorn maker

Procedure:

1. Discuss with the children how the Indians enjoyed corn in many forms—whole, dried, and ground into flour. Explain that they also made popcorn by heating corn in hand-made pottery jars over a fire, a process they taught to the Pilgrim children.
2. Make popcorn with the children and enjoy it as a snack. Follow the instructions that come with the popcorn maker. (**Caution:** Be sure the children stay away from the hot popcorn maker.) Let the children help measure the popcorn and add the salt and butter.

Variations/Ways to Extend:

- Show pictures of foods that the Indians taught the Pilgrims to grow and harvest. These include tomatoes, white potatoes, corn, squash, sweet potatoes, and wild rice.
- Play the song "Popcorn's Popping" from the album *Science in a Nutshell: Songs Exploring Science Experiences for the Early Years (Preschool–Grade 2)*. This is available from Kimbo Educational, 86 South 5th Avenue, Long Branch, NJ 07740.
- Teach the children the following rhyme and act it out:

  I'm a popcorn kernel in a pot, (*squat down and curl up*)
    Heat me up and watch me pop. (*jump up*)
  When I get all puffed up, I am done (*jump up again*)
    Popping corn is so much fun. (*jump up and down several times*)

Weekly Subtheme: Thanksgiving

II–51 ONCE THERE WAS A PILGRIM

Subject Area: Language Arts

Concepts/Skills: Repeats a simple fingerplay
Uses *me* correctly

Objective: The children will demonstrate the actions to the fingerplay.

Material: • Words to the fingerplay

Procedure:

1. Teach the following fingerplay to the children:

> I knew a pilgrim (*extend one finger up*)
>   Who tried every way (*nod head*)
> To catch a turkey (*raise other hand and spread fingers*)
>   For Thanksgiving day.
> He said "caught you" to the turkey (*make a catching motion*)
>   He said "caught you" to the hen (*make a catching motion*)
> He said "caught you" to the pumpkin (*make a catching motion*)
>   He said "caught you" to me! (*point at self*)
> Well, he caught that turkey
>   And he caught that hen
> He even caught the pumpkin (*hold hands close to body*)
>   But he didn't catch me! (*shake head no and point to self*)

2. Repeat the fingerplay several times with the children.

Variation/Way to Extend:

• Use props, such as Pilgrim hats, paper turkeys, and pumpkins, to enhance the fingerplay.

II–52   TURKEY ROUND-UP

Subject Area: Gross Motor Game

Concepts/Skills: Follows directions
Develops gross motor movement of running

Objective: The children will play a Thanksgiving tag game.

Material: • Chalk or tape

Procedure:

1. In a large open area, choose one child to be a Pilgrim while the other children are turkeys.
2. Pretend that there is a forest on one side of the area where the turkeys stand. Mark off this area by a line to show that it is a safety area for turkeys.
3. Have the Pilgrim start out on the opposite side, gobbling like a turkey to fool the turkeys. Tell the turkeys that they are fooled so they come out to eat the crumbs the Pilgrim has pretended to scatter.
4. Then have the Pilgrim yell "Thanksgiving" and try to catch some turkeys. The turkeys run back to the forest, but those tagged become Pilgrims also.
5. Continue until all turkeys are caught or until the time is over.

Variations/Ways to Extend:

• Read *Thank You, You're Welcome* by Louis Slobodkin (New York: Vanguard, 1957).
• Read *Thanksgiving at the Tappletons* by Eileen Spinelli (Reading, MA: Addison-Wesley, 1982).

Weekly Subtheme: Thanksgiving

II–53 PAPER TURKEYS

Subject Area: Art

Concepts/Skills: Uses scissors
Develops fine motor movement of pasting

Objective: The children will construct paper turkeys.

Materials:
- Pre-cut turkey shapes (see pattern)
- Colored paper
- Paste
- Scissors

Procedure:

1. Give each child a pre-cut turkey shape.
2. Have the children cut strips of colored paper for turkey feathers.
3. Have the children use their index fingers to apply paste to the feathers. Tell them to paste the feathers all across the back of the turkey shape and some down the side for a wing.

Variation/Way to Extend:

- Read *Little Bear's Thanksgiving* by Else H. Minarik (New York: Harper and Row, 1960).

II-54   THANKSGIVING HIDE AND SEEK

Subject Area: Math

Concepts/Skills: Rote counts from 1 to 5
Becomes familiar with Thanksgiving symbols

Objective: The children will play a counting game related to Thanksgiving.

Materials: • An assortment of small Thanksgiving objects

Procedure:

1.   Have a child hide a small holiday object—such as a little Pilgrim doll, small turkey, candle, cornucopia, or toy Indian canoe—while the other children close their eyes and slowly count to five aloud with you.
2.   Then have the children look for the object while the child who hid it counts to five slowly.
3.   Whoever finds the first object gets to hide the next object. If no one finds it, have the child who hid it tell where it is and take another turn.

Variation/Way to Extend:

• Use the objects to also discuss shape, color, and size.

II–55 CRANBERRY CUPCAKES

Subject Area: Nutrition and Foods Experience

Concepts/Skills: Demonstrates accurate sense of sight, taste, touch, and smell
Measures and pours

Objective: The children will participate in baking a holiday food.

Materials:
- 2 cups flour
- 1 cup sugar (or honey equivalent)
- 1½ teaspoons baking powder
- 1 teaspoon salt
- ¼ teaspoon butter (at room temperature)
- 2 cups whole cranberries
- ¾ cup orange juice
- 1 egg
- Walnuts (optional)
- Bowl
- Wooden spoon
- Oven
- Cupcake tins

Procedure:

1. Combine the four dry ingredients in a bowl. Cut in the butter. Stir together and add the orange juice and egg. Mix together and add the whole cranberries.
2. Grease the cupcake tins and bake at 350° F. for about twenty to twenty-five minutes or until done. (**Caution:** Be sure the children stay away from the heat.)

Variation/Way to Extend:

- Pour the cupcake batter into decorative miniature muffin paper cups for an especially festive look and a size of which the children are fond.

THE SPIRIT OF THE SEASON

○ Giving and Sharing

○ Holiday Games

○ Children Around the World

○ Holiday Foods and Traditions

Weekly Subtheme: Giving and Sharing

II–56 HOLIDAY MOBILE

Subject Area: Art

Concepts/Skills: Pastes with index finger
Holds crayon properly

Objective: The children will create mobiles to give as gifts.

Materials:
- Twigs
- String or fishline
- Stapler
- Crayons
- White spray paint
- Glue
- Glitter
- Paper scraps
- Pre-cut paper holiday shapes

Procedure:

1. Take a winter walk with the children and gather a twig for each child.

2. Then spray paint each twig white.

3. When the twigs are dry, assist the children in gluing a bit of glitter on each one.

4. Have each child then choose three shapes from an assortment of pre-cut paper holiday shapes. On these, ask the children to color and paste paper scraps.

5. Tie three strands of fishline or string onto each twig.

6. Staple a decorated shape onto the end of each line and have the children give these mobiles as gifts to friends or relatives.

Variations/Ways to Extend:
- Pre-cut easel paper into large triangle shapes to form evergreen trees. Have the children paint these trees with the understanding that they will be used to decorate the classroom.
- Read *The Giving Tree* by Shel Silverstein (New York: Harper and Row, 1964).

II-57   CIRCLE JUMP

Subject Area: Gross Motor Game

Concepts/Skills: Walks forward
Follows two directions

Objective: The children will play a game by responding in pairs to the teacher's commands.

Materials:
- Words to a holiday song
- Rope
- Sleigh bells (optional)

Procedure:

1. With a long rope, create a circle approximately six feet in diameter.

2. Pair the children and ask them to hold hands while walking around the outside of the circle as you clap your hands or shake sleigh bells and sing a popular holiday song, such as "Jingle Bells."

3. When you stop clapping, the children (still holding hands) must together jump inside the circle to avoid being tagged by you.

Variation/Way to Extend:

- Ask the children to crawl, tiptoe, or jump around the circle.

Weekly Subtheme: Giving and Sharing

II–58 PAPER CUP COLORS

Subject Areas: Science and Social Studies

Concepts/Skills: Points to the appropriate color upon command
Enjoys being with other children

Objectives: The children will be able to identify colors and share treats.

Materials:
- Six paper cups
- Colored paper circles
- Glue
- Treats (cookies, balloons, stickers)

Procedure:

1. Turn six papers cups upside down. On the bottom of each cup, glue a different colored circle, one each of the following colors: blue, orange, purple, red, green, and yellow. Place two treats under each cup.

2. Name a color and ask a child to point to the color named. When the correct color is chosen, the child receives both treats under that cup and is asked to find someone else with whom he or she would like to sit down and share the goodies. (Provide extra treats for those who would prefer not to share.)

Variations/Ways to Extend:

- Teach shape identification, letter recognition, and numeral recognition using the same procedure.
- Read *Little Blue & Little Yellow* by Leo Lionni (New York: Astor-Honor, 1959).
- Read the poem "Now in December" (anonymous). This is found in *Hello Year,* poems selected by Leland Jacobs (Champaign, IL: Garrard, 1972).

Weekly Subtheme: Giving and Sharing

II–59 SHARING COOKIES

Subject Area: Math

Concepts/Skills: Matches shapes
Follows two directions

Objectives: The children will make cookies and enjoy these with friends while playing a shape game.

Materials:
- Refrigerator-cookie dough
- Cookie sheets
- Drinking glass
- Rolling pin
- Scissors
- Half sheets of construction paper prepared with shapes
- Phonograph
- Knife
- Oven
- Hole punch
- Glue
- String
- Holiday album

Procedure:

1. Make angel cookies with the children by rolling some refrigerator-cookie dough. Cut circles by pressing the glass into the dough, and then cut these in half to make the wings. Use a triangle shape for the body and a circle for the head.

2. Bake the cookies according to the package's directions. (**Caution:** Be sure the children stay away from the heat.)

3. Distribute the half sheets of colored construction paper that have been prepared with either a square, rectangle, triangle, or circle glued on each sheet. Make two or three sets, depending on the number of children in the group.

4. Place a string through each sheet and tie it loosely around a child's neck.

5. Give each child one cookie. Play a holiday song on the phonograph and ask the children to walk in a circle while listening to the music. When the music stops, each child looks for someone else wearing the same shape as the one he or she is wearing.

6. When matched, the children sit down together and eat their cookies.

Variations/Ways to Extend:

- Let the children paint the unbaked cookies by mixing evaporated milk with food coloring and applying the cookie paint with small brushes reserved solely for this purpose. Bake and enjoy.
- For background music, you might select "Santa Claus Is Comin' to Town" from *Pops Goes Christmas* by Arthur Fiedler/Boston Pops (RCA Records).

Weekly Subtheme: Giving and Sharing

II-60 RUDOLPH PUPPET

Subject Area: Language Arts

Concepts/Skills: Develops fine motor skills of tracing, pasting, and using scissors
Listens to short stories

Objectives: The children will construct reindeer puppets and describe how Rudolph helped Santa.

Materials:
- Story of Rudolph the Red-Nosed Reindeer
- One brown lunch bag for each child
- Precut black eyes and red noses
- Black construction paper
- Pencils
- White chalk
- Scissors
- Glue

Procedure:

1. Read the story of Rudolph the Red-Nosed Reindeer. Explain how Rudolph shared himself and his light to help Santa Claus.

2. Give each child a piece of black construction paper. Using the white chalk, assist each child in tracing both hands on the paper. Cut out the hand shapes, which will be used as antlers.

3. Give each child a lunch bag and distribute the facial features to be glued into place along with the antlers. Suggest to the children that they color white spots on the bag with the chalk.

4. When the glue has dried, tell the story again and let them use their puppets to hold up and act out the reindeer parts. Ask them how Rudolph gave of himself to help Santa.

Variations/Ways to Extend:
- Make only one Rudolph with a red nose. Make all the others with black noses. As the story is told, share Rudolph by letting the children take turns being the red-nosed Rudolph.
- Play the song "Rudolph the Red-Nosed Reindeer—Finale" (sung by Burl Ives) from the album *Original Sound Track and Music from Rudolph the Red-Nosed Reindeer* (MCA Records).
- Once the children are familiar with the words to the song, play the instrumental version on Side Two of the album and encourage them to sing along.

II-61   SANTA, SANTA, YOUR PRESENT IS GONE!

Subject Area: Social Studies

Concept/Skill: Begins learning the "give and take" of play

Objective: The children take turns looking for a holiday present.

Materials: • Cardboard box decorated as a present
  • Santa's hat
  • Blindfold

Procedure:

1.   Select one child to be Santa Claus and ask him or her to wear the hat.

2.   Show the children the "present" and tell them that "this present fell off Santa's sled and he has to look for it."

3.   While Santa is blindfolded and seated with his or her back to the other children, place the gift somewhere in the room.

4.   Remove the blindfold from Santa and ask the child to search for the lost present. As Santa gets closer to the present, have the children say, "Happy Holidays."

5.   Once the present is found, let another child have a turn at playing Santa.

Variations/Ways to Extend:

• Put a snack of peanuts, raisins, carob chips, and small marshmallows into the decorated cardboard box. When the game is concluded, open the present and share the snack.

• Use the Caldecott Medal book *The Rooster Crows* by Maud and Miska Petersham (New York: Macmillan, 1969). Originally published in 1945, it is a collection of rhymes, fingerplays, and games from days past.

II-62   HOLIDAY COLORS

Subject Area: Gross Motor Game

Concepts/Skills: Points to appropriate color upon command
Moves body in response to simple teacher command
Understands the prepositions *in, on,* and *off*

Objectives: The children will identify the colors of the season and participate in a gross motor game.

Materials:
- Nine beanbags (three red, three white, and three green)
- Tambourine
- Red, green, and white holiday objects

Procedure:

1. Talk to the children about the colors red, green, and white being important to the holiday season. Ask the children, "What are some red things you see this time of year?" (bows, berries, lights, candles) "What are some white things you see this time of year?" (snow, snowmen, candles, popcorn) "What are some green things you see this time of year?" (holly, wreaths, trees). Provide some of these objects for the children to handle.

2. Spread the nine beanbags (three of each color) around on the floor. Ask the children to sit on the floor and select three children at a time to participate.

3. Using a tambourine, sound out a slow beat that allows the children to walk around the beanbags in a circle. As the children walk, give such directions as, "When the beat stops, place your foot on a red beanbag." "When the beat stops, place your elbow on a white beanbag." "When the beat stops, place your knee on a green beanbag."

4. Continue with other directions using other parts of the body. Encourage the children to enjoy the humorous aspects of their positions if you combine two directions at one time. Also have the children try to walk while balancing beanbags on their heads.

Variation/Way to Extend:
- Use red and green large hoops or circles of heavy yarn taped to the floor. Say such directions as, "When the beat stops, place your body inside the hoop."

II-63 HOLIDAY MYSTERY BAG

Subject Area: Thinking Game

Concepts/Skills: Demonstrates accurate sense of touch
Speaks in four- to six-word sentences

Objective: The children will describe objects through the feeling of touch.

Materials:
- Objects that pertain to the holiday season (twigs from evergreen trees, ribbon, yarn, tinsel, pine cones, wrapping paper, ornaments, and so on)
- Large paper bag

Procedure:

1. Ask the children to identify the objects you have assembled or collected as a group. Let the children touch and feel each item as you explain its use or significance to the season.

2. Place all the objects in a large paper "mystery bag."

3. Have each child take a turn reaching in and grasping an object to feel and identify (either by describing it or naming it).

Variations/Ways to Extend:

- Create a group collage by gluing the materials from the mystery bag onto a sheet of oaktag.
- Prepare several small film canisters by filling each with an item that possesses a strong scent reminiscent of the season, such as cinnamon, pine needles, cloves, a small candy cane, ginger, or an orange slice. Let each child take a turn sniffing and experiencing the aroma of each item.
- Serve gingerbread cookies with milk or juice at snack time.

II–64   WHERE HAS SANTA GONE?

Subject Area: Math

Concepts/Skills: Rote counts to 10
Speaks a four-word sentence

Objectives: The children will play a hide-and-seek game and demonstrate counting from 1 to 10.

Material: • One piece of a Santa Claus costume

Procedure:

1.   Ask one child to wear the one piece of costume, such as a cap or beard.

2.   Have the other children cover their eyes and as a group (with your assistance) count from 1 to 10 while Santa finds a hiding place. Note: This game, which is based on "Hide and Seek," is best played in a large room or outside—weather permitting, of course.

3.   When the children finish counting, have them begin their search for Santa. Encourage the children to verbalize when they find him or her, saying, "I found Santa Claus."

Variations/Ways to Extend:

•   With each turn, encourage the children to count one number higher—that is, to 11, then 12, and so on.

•   For background music this week, play a recording of "The Ball" from *Children's Games* by Georges Bizet.

II-65   RUDOLPH, RUDOLPH, REINDEER

Subject Area: Music

Concepts/Skills: Participates in a group
Repeats a simple song

Objectives: The children will sing a song and follow directions.

Material: • Words to the song

Procedure:

1. Review the song "Rudolph the Red-Nosed Reindeer" with the children.

2. Gather the children in a circle and play the game "Rudolph, Rudolph, Reindeer" (a version of "Duck, Duck, Goose").

3. Have one child move clockwise around the outside of the circle while tapping the children on the head and saying "Rudolph" each time he or she taps a child. As soon as the child taps someone and says "Reindeer," the tapped child gets up and becomes the chaser, attempting to tag the other child before he or she runs completely around the outside of the circle, returns to the vacated spot, and sits down in it. The child who is not seated now moves around the outside of the circle saying, "Rudolph, Rudolph, Reindeer" as each head is tapped.

4. Continue the game following the same procedure.

Variation/Way to Extend:

• Let each child paint his or her own version of Rudolph the Red-Nosed Reindeer at the easels.

II-66 FAMILIES AROUND THE WORLD

Subject Area: Social Studies

Concept/Skill: Understands that people are alike and different in how they look and feel

Objective: The children will observe pictures of people from Mexico, Japan, and France.

Materials:
- Pictures of family customs
- Scissors
- Clear self-stick vinyl
- Cardboard

Procedure:

1. Write the Information Center on Children's Cultures, Committee for UNICEF, 331 East 38th Street, New York, NY 10016. Ask for free pictures of family customs in Mexico, Japan, and France. (Calendars and festival figures are also available for a small fee.)

2. Mount the pictures on cardboard and laminate them with clear self-stick vinyl.

3. Select one picture from each country and discuss each one with the children. See what similarities to their own families the children may discover. Discuss how people may look different from people we know but may still have the same needs and feelings (clothing, food, housing, joy, love, and so on).

Variation/Way to Extend:

- Place three carpet strips (8 feet long, 4 inches wide) on the floor with pictures from families around the world at the end of each strip. Have the children walk the strips to each picture and tell how the people pictured are feeling and why they might be feeling this way.

II-67   GUACAMOLE DIP

Subject Area: Nutrition and Food Experience

Concepts/Skills: Develops gross motor movements of mashing and stirring
Demonstrates accurate sense of taste and smell

Objective: The children will help prepare a nutritious Mexican snack.

Materials:
- Two avocados
- Tomato
- Small onion
- One garlic clove
- Salt
- Pepper
- Lemon juice
- Washed and cut pieces of carrots, radishes, cucumbers, broccoli, and celery
- Fork
- Knife
- Bowl

Procedure:

1. Ask the children to help identify each of the ingredients and have them repeat their names.

2. Make a cut around the avocados with a knife, split them in half, and remove the large seeds.

3. Let the children help mash the avocados in a bowl with a fork.

4. Chop the tomato, mince the onion and the garlic, and add these to the mashed avocado. Sprinkle with a little lemon juice, add a dash of salt and pepper, and let the children stir.

5. Serve with the fresh vegetables for a spicy, nutritious snack.

Variation/Way to Extend:

- Use the avocado seeds to start window plants. Partially submerge the seed in water in a jar and watch the roots as well as the leaves grow. Although it takes a long time to get started, the plant may survive for ten years or more.

II–68   MAKING MARACAS

Subject Area: Art

Concepts/Skills: Listens to directions
Holds crayons with fingers
Points to yellow, red, and orange

Objectives: The children will construct maracas and pretend to march in a mariachi band.

Materials:
- Tennis ball or potato chip cans with plastic lids
- Stones
- Paper
- Crayons
- Small dowels or tongue depressors
- Masking tape
- Knife
- Glue
- Sequins
- Mariachi music

Procedure:

1. Explain to the children that during the holiday season in Mexico, mariachi bands stroll the streets and play their trumpets, violins, guitars, and maracas. Their music is lively and gay.

2. Tell the children that they are going to make maracas.

3. Using tennis ball or potato chip cans with plastic lids, first decorate the outside of the can by having the children identify and use red, orange, and yellow crayons on paper. Glue these papers carefully onto the cans. Glue some sequins to the covered cans to add a special dash to the designs.

4. Partially fill the cans with small stones.

5. Cut a small hole in each lid and attach a small dowel or tongue depressor for a handle. Tape the stick to the lid and then the lid to the can.

6. Play a little mariachi music for the children to enjoy. Ask the children to listen for the maracas.

Variations/Ways to Extend:
- Allow the children to march as a mariachi band, playing their maracas.
- Add other instruments to the mariachi band: a cardboard paper towel roll can be a horn; metal measuring spoons can be shakers; a wooden bowl and spoon can give rhythm; and rubber from an inner tube stretched across a five-pound coffee can's mouth and held in place by a thick rubber band can be a drum.

II-69   RICE SOUP

Subject Areas: Language Arts and Nutrition

Concepts/Skills: Develops fine motor movements of measuring and pouring
Observes how to keep up with time by watching the clock

Objectives: The children will identify the ingredients in the rice soup and enjoy the finished product.

Materials:
- Picture
- 1 cup long grain white rice
- 4 cups beef bouillon
- ½ cup diced potato
- ½ cup diced celery
- ½ cup diced carrot
- ¼ cup diced onion
- Large pot and cover
- Stove or other heat source
- Bowls
- Spoons
- Napkins

Procedure:

1. Show pictures of Japanese children eating. These are available free from the Japan Information Center, Consultate General of Japan, 18th Floor, 299 Park Avenue, New York, NY 10171. Tell the children that around the holidays in Japan, a flat, rice-filled cake called *mochi* is made.

2. Tell the children that they are going to make a nutritious rice soup.

3. Place the bouillon, potato, celery, carrot, and onion in a large pot. See if the children can identify each ingredient as it is placed in the pot.

4. Cover the pot and simmer it for 30 minutes. (**Caution:** Be sure the children stay away from the heat source.)

5. Add the rice to the pot and cook for twenty minutes more.

6. Serve the soup in small bowls as a snack. Ask the children to notice what has happened to each ingredient after it has been cooked. Ask the children to use one or two words to tell how each part of the soup looks now.

Variation/Way to Extend:
- Read *Stone Soup* by Marcia Brown (New York: Scribner's, 1947).

II–70 HAT DANCE

Subject Area: Music

Concepts/Skills: Repeats a simple song
Participates with enthusiasm

Objective: The children will participate in a game song about hats from other cultures.

Materials:
• Words and music to the song
• Pictures
• Sombrero, beret, and turban

Procedure:

1. Show the children pictures of people doing a Mexican hat dance. Talk about what the dancers do (stamp, dance, twirl, circle, but never step on the hat).

2. Teach the children to sing "Hat Dance."

3. Place the sombrero, beret, and turban on the floor in the center of the circle of children. Let each child do a "hat dance" as everyone sings "Hat Dance."

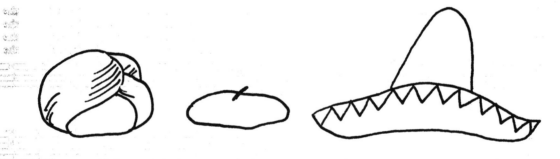

Variations/Ways to Extend:

• Allow the children to move around each hat in different ways. They might hop over, walk backward, roll, crawl, and so on.
• Play a recording of the "Mexican Hat Dance" and let the children dance to it. One version is called "Jarabe Tapatio" from the album *Children's Songs of Mexico*. It is published by Bowmar Publications, a part of Belwin-Mills Publishing Company, Melville, NY 11747.

Hat Dance

Words and Music by **BOB MESSANO**
Arranged by John Sheehan

1. Can you do a hat dance?_____

Can you dance a round?_____ Go 'round and 'round the
2. Go 'round and 'round the
3. Go 'round and 'round the
4. Go 'round and 'round the

big som - bre - ro and turn it up - side down!_____
French be - ret and turn it up - side down!_____
pret - ty tur - ban and turn it up - side down!_____
old straw hat and turn it up - side down!_____

II–71 DRAMATIZING CHRISTMAS DAY

Subject Area: Creative Dramatics

Concept/Skill: Dramatizes a simple story

Objectives: The children will listen to a story and participate in dramatizing the story.

Materials:
- Props
- Book

Procedure:

1. Read *A Christmas Book* by Joan W. Anglund (New York: Random, 1983). Specifically read the section entitled "A Very Special Day."

2. Prepare the props (pillows, blanket, doll house, teddy bears, table, and utensils) that are discussed in the story.

3. Select six children and read the story again, this time assisting the children in dramatizing each scene. When time is available, allow the others to take turns acting out the story.

Variations/Ways to Extend:

- Encourage the children to talk during different events (opening presents, eating dinner) within the story.
- Play a recording of "March of the Toys." (Refer to *Music to Have Fun By* by the National Orchestra, Howard Mitchell, conductor, RCA Records.)

II–72 MAKING EGGNOG

Subject Area: Nutrition and Food Experience

Concepts/Skills: Demonstrates sense of smell and taste
Follows directions in sequence

Objective: The children will participate in mixing ingredients to make eggnog.

Materials:
- 4 eggs
- Nutmeg or cinnamon
- Vanilla
- Vanilla ice cream
- Milk
- Small cups
- Bowl
- Small strainer
- Measuring spoons
- Measuring cup
- Blender

Procedure:

1. Tell the children that they are going to make eggnog, a traditional holiday drink. Be sure to let the children identify, smell, beat, measure, and pour the ingredients.

2. Beat four eggs and pour through a strainer into a bowl. Add half a teaspoon of vanilla. Add and stir in one cup of milk and two scoops of vanilla ice cream. Pour into a blender and mix for thirty seconds. Pour the eggnog into individual cups.

3. Sprinkle nutmeg or cinnamon on top of each serving and let the children enjoy the eggnog at snack time.

4. Ask the children if the eggnog tastes sweet or salty. Ask, "What words tell how it tastes?" (*yummy, delicious, cold, good,* and so on).

Variations/Ways to Extend:

- Count the number of cups of eggnog that are filled.
- For extra goodness, add a mashed banana to the ingredients. Let the children help mash the banana before blending.

II–73   CARRYING SANTA'S TOYS

Subject Area: Gross Motor Game

Concepts/Skills: Walks forward on a line
Jumps three times with both feet

Objective: The children will demonstrate gross motor movements while traveling through an obstacle course.

Materials:
- Equipment listed under "Procedure"
- White pillowcase filled with pretend presents
- Santa's beard or hat

Procedure:

1.   Tell the children that each of them is going to pretend to be Santa Claus's helper by taking his bag of toys to him.

2.   Construct an obstacle course by placing the following items around the room:

    a large sturdy cardboard box open at both ends
    a small chair to climb over
    masking-tape shapes on the floor to jump on with both feet
    a small table to crawl under
    blocks to step over
    masking tape strips to walk on
    string hung from two chairs to step over

3.   Have each child carry a white pillowcase fitted with two or three empty boxes decorated as presents as he or she negotiates his or her way through the course.

4.   Wear a Santa hat or beard and congratulate each child upon completion of the obstacle course for safely getting the presents to you.

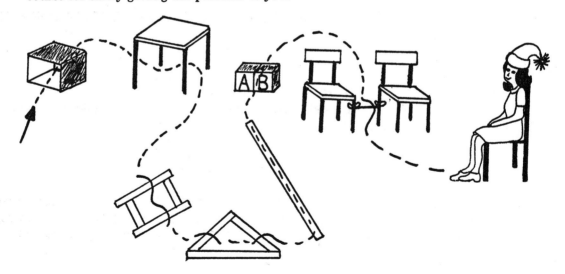

Variation/Way to Extend:

- Reverse the obstacle course. Have the children travel from the last piece of equipment to the first.

II–74 TREE DECORATIONS

Subject Area: Art

Concepts/Skills: Points to colors upon command
Pastes
Holds crayons with fingers

Objectives: The children will construct tree decorations and play a game.

Materials:
- Oaktag
- Construction paper
- Crayons
- Paints
- Brushes
- Glitter
- Glue
- Tape
- Scissors

Procedure:

1. Cut out a large Christmas tree from green oaktag. Tape the tree to the lower part of a wall so that the children can reach it.

2. Tell the children that they are going to make paper decorations that can be taped onto the tree.

3. Cut circles from white construction paper and have the children decorate them. Ask the children to identify the colors as they are used.

4. Pre-cut shapes to look like light bulbs. Allow the children to decorate these with glue and various colors of glitter. Again, ask the children to identify the colors as they are used.

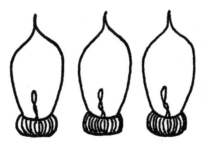

5. Have the children play a variation of "Pin the Tail on the Donkey." Place pieces of tape on each decoration and ask the children to close their eyes while they try to tape the decoration onto the paper tree. (Note: You may have to help lead each child to the tree.)

Variation/Way to Extend:

- Make three-dimensional decorations by painting styrofoam balls, making paper chains, using papier-mâché, and so on. (Note: Use white glue mixed with poster paint so that it will adhere to the styrofoam.)

II–75 GINGERBREAD PEOPLE

Subject Areas: Language Arts and Food Experience

Concepts/Skills: Demonstrates sense of smell and taste
Develops fine motor movements of blending, rolling, mixing, and measuring

Objectives: The children will identify the materials needed and proceed to make gingerbread people.

Materials:
- This recipe makes fifteen four-inch cookies
- ½ cup shortening
- ½ cup sugar
- ½ cup dark molasses
- ¼ cup water
- 2½ cups unbleached flour
- ¾ teaspoon salt
- ½ teaspoon baking soda
- ¾ teaspoon ginger
- ¼ teaspoon nutmeg
- ⅛ teaspoon allspice
- Raisins, candied cherries, walnut pieces, citron, string licorice cut into small pieces, and decorator's icing
- Cookie sheets
- Rolling pin and cloth
- Large bowl
- Measuring cup and spoons
- Oven
- Gingerbread girl/boy cookie cutters

Procedure:

1. While preparing the cookies, ask the children to name the utensils and ingredients as they are used. Have the children smell and compare the spice scents. Also let them take turns measuring, mixing, rolling, cutting, and decorating the cookies.

2. Cream the shortening and sugar. Blend in the molasses, water, flour, salt, soda, ginger, nutmeg, and allspice. Cover. Chill two to three hours or use with the class the next day.

3. Heat the oven to 375° F. **(Caution:** Be sure the children stay away from the heat.) Roll the dough to a ¼″ thickness on a lightly floured cloth. Cut with gingerbread girl/boy cookie cutters. Place them on an ungreased baking sheet. Press raisins into the dough for eyes, noses, and buttons. Use bits of candied cherries, citron, and licorice for other trim.

4. Bake for ten to twelve minutes. Immediately remove the cookies from the cookie sheets and cool.

5. Trim with decorator's icing.

Variations/Ways to Extend:

- Make a hole through the top of each cookie so that it can be hung as an ornament.

- Read *The Mole Family's Christmas* by Russell Hoban (New York: Scholastic, 1980; reprint of 1969 Four Winds edition).

WINTER

- ○ Getting a Fresh Start
- ○ Health and Safety
- ○ Snow
- ○ Water and Ice

II-76 NEW YEAR'S PARTY!

Subject Areas: Social Studies and Nutrition

Concepts/Skills: Follows directions
Understands concept of a new year

Objectives: The children will celebrate the new year by making and eating nutritious snacks.

Materials:
- Apples
- Peanut butter
- Cantaloupe
- Seedless grapes
- Mandarin oranges
- Fruit cocktail
- Miniature marshmallows
- Bananas
- Shredded coconut
- Eggnog
- Knife
- Forks
- Paper plates
- Napkins
- Cups

Procedure:

1. Provide a variety of snack foods for the children to help prepare by following your directions. Peel, core, and slice some apples and have the children spread peanut butter on them. Slice a cantaloupe and line the curved wedges with seedless grapes. Make a fruit salad from chilled fruit cocktail, orange slices, miniature marshmallows, sliced bananas, and shredded coconut.

2. Buy or make some eggnog (see activity II-72) to drink.

3. Arrange everything in an attractive display so that the children may make their selections.

Variation/Way to Extend:

- Decorate the room festively, perhaps with some red balloons for the children to take home. Display a new calendar and pictures of New Year's Eve and New Year's Day celebrations (parties, parades, sports events).

Weekly Subtheme: Getting a Fresh Start

II–77 HAPPY NEW YEAR SONG

Subject Areas: Music and Art

Concepts/Skills: Memorizes and repeats a simple song
Engages in simple conversation
Paints with a large brush

Objectives: The children will sing a song, discuss the new year, and create a painting.

Materials:
- Words to the song
- Easel paper
- Paints
- Brushes

Procedure:

1. Teach the children the song "Happy New Year," sung to the tune of "Happy Birthday to You."

   Happy New Year to you,
   Happy New Year to you,
   Happy New Year everybody,
   Happy New Year to you.

2. After the song, discuss with the children things that they can do right now to begin having fun and learning new things in the new year. Ask the children what they would like to learn about or learn how to do, such as, "Who would like to learn how to skip?" "Who would like to learn how to catch a big ball?" "Who would like to make more paintings?" "Who would like to sing more songs?"

3. Use the children's interests to plan further activities. Let the children try out some of their ideas now. Let them creatively express these ideas with paints at the easel. Remember: Do not expect results to be truly representational. Simply accept and appropriately commend each child's efforts.

Variations/Ways to Extend:

- Read *The Things I Like* by Françoise (New York: Scribner's, 1960).
- Let the children engage in some dramatic play using the ideas they expressed in the activity.

Weekly Subtheme: Getting a Fresh Start

II–78   WINTER PRINT

Subject Area: Art

Concepts/Skills: Explores a new medium
Expresses self creatively

Objective: The children will create a print using pine boughs.

Materials:
- Pine boughs
- Pie tins
- White paint
- Dark blue or black paper
- Mica flakes
- Background music

Procedure:

1. Go on a winter walk with the children and collect one or two small boughs from nearby pine trees. Be sure each child has a small pine spray with which to work.

2. Fill several pie tins with white paint and distribute sheets of dark blue or black construction paper.

3. Have the children dip their boughs into the paint and print a design on the paper. Then have them sprinkle the design with crushed mica flakes.

4. You might want to play background music to encourage a relaxed, expressive atmosphere. Try some selections from *Snow Drops* by Tchaikovsky.

Variation/Way to Extend:

- Let the children explore various white media on dark paper. Let them experiment with white chalk, white crayons, and white oil-based chalk on a sheet of dark blue or black construction paper.

II-79 THE COLOR TREE

Subject Areas: Math and Art

Concepts/Skills: Names three primary colors
Points to and labels triangle shape
Copies horizontal and diagonal lines
Paints with a large brush

Objectives: The children will draw and paint an evergreen tree.

Materials:
- Crayons
- Red, blue, and yellow paints
- Paper
- Brushes

Procedure:

1. Work individually at first to help each child copy the lines needed to make a large triangle for an evergreen tree design. Using crayons, have the child copy the horizontal line, then the two diagonal lines, and finally the base.

2. Have the child make two more diagonal lines to create three divisions of space in the tree.

3. Let the children use red, blue, and yellow paints to make each section a different color.

Variations/Ways to Extend:

- For a snack, drink red cranberry juice and sprinkle blueberries over yellow custard. Ask the children to name the colors.
- Read *Red Is for Apples* by Beth G. Hoffman (New York: Random, 1966).

II–80   SUMMER IS HOT/WINTER IS COLD

Subject Area: Language Arts

Concept/Skill: Understands opposites (up/down, fast/slow, open/closed, hot/cold, stop/go, big/little, happy/sad)

Objectives: The children will describe and demonstrate words that are opposite.

Materials:
- Water bottle
- Very warm water
- Cup of ice
- Records
- Record player
- Pictures
- Bell or other instrument

Procedure:

1. Discuss with the children the idea of a year and seasons. Do this by helping them to recall holidays and what the weather was like at the time. For example, the Fourth of July is usually a hot day and is associated with parades.

2. Help the children to recall characteristics of the summer and compare these with those of the winter season. Use the opportunity to emphasize these opposites: summer was *hot,* winter is *cold.*

3. Use a water bottle filled with very warm water to let the children touch something hot. Show them a cup of ice to compare hot with cold.

4. Talk about and show pictures of other opposites. Use movement to demonstrate as many of these as possible. For example, have the children jump *up* and go *down. Open* their hands and *close* them. *Open* their eyes and *close* them. Use a bell or other instrument as a signal and have the children *go* when you ring it once and *stop* when you ring it twice. Use music and dancing to denote *fast* and *slow.* Have them make *happy* and *sad* faces into a mirror. Sort pictures of *big* and *little* objects into two boxes, and find some examples around the room.

Variations/Ways to Extend:

- Read *Heavy Is a Hippopotamus* by Miriam Schlein (Reading, MA: Addison-Wesley, 1954).
- Further illustrate the concept of opposites by playing a classical music piece and having the children carefully note the tempo (fast/slow) of the music. A good selection is Mozart's Piano Concerto in C Major, K.467.
- Vary this activity to suit your climatic conditions.

II–81   A VISIT TO THE DOCTOR

Subject Area: Creative Dramatics and Movement

Concepts/Skills: Cooperates in a group
Plays with symbols

Objective: The children will use medical props to dramatize a visit to the doctor.

Materials:
- Gauze
- Tape
- Bandages
- Tongue depressors
- Cotton balls
- String
- Cardboard boxes or crates
- Egg carton for sorting
- Used syringes (no needles)
- Toy blood pressure kit
- Toy stethoscope
- Flashlights
- Stuffed animals

Procedure:

1. Discuss how doctors and nurses work to keep us well and help us to get better when we are ill. Remind the children that women can be doctors and men can be nurses.

2. Provide as many pieces of medical paraphernalia as possible for the children to role play being doctors, nurses, and patients.

3. Guide the activity enough to help the children understand how and why some of this equipment is used. Encourage dramatic play using stuffed animals as patients, too. Use cardboard boxes or crates as ambulances.

Variations/Ways to Extend:

- Contact the supply room at your local hospital and ask if anything is available for your use.
- Read *Tommy Goes to the Doctor* (Boston: Houghton Mifflin, 1972) or *Betsy and the Doctor* (New York: Random, 1978), both by Gunilla Wolde.

Weekly Subtheme: Health and Safety

II–82   RELAX YOURSELF

Subject Area: Science

Concepts/Skills: Feels good about self and abilities
Names body parts

Objective: The children will practice relaxation exercises.

Materials: • Large open area
• Mats

Procedure:

1. Explain to the children that rest and relaxation are important to our bodies. They help our bodies get strong again and can help us when we are upset or tense.

2. Dim the lights and do some slow, deep breathing while sitting on the mats.

3. Ask everyone to lie down and close their eyes. Direct the children to tighten up and then relax the muscles in various areas of the body. Begin at the face and work your way down through the torso and limbs to the toes.

Variations/Ways to Extend:

• Enhance the mood for this activity by playing some soft instrumental music in the background. One example is Tchaikovsky's "Waltz of the Flowers" from the Nutcracker Ballet, found on the album *Children's Introduction to Classical Music* (Peter Pan Records).

• Another album excellent for enhancing quiet time is *Follow the Clouds—Music and Narration for Rest Time Reflection* (Melody House Publishing Company). It combines classical music pieces by Strauss, Debussy, Brahms, and others with narration that evokes images that are comforting and familiar to children.

IJ-83   WINTER CLOTHES

Subject Area: Language Arts

Concept/Skill: Recognizes and names articles of clothing worn

Objective: The children will list articles of clothing necessary for the cold winter season.

Materials:
- Flannelboard
- Felt cutouts (see patterns on next page)
- Pictures

Procedure:

1. Discuss the elements of winter (cold temperatures, rain, sleet, snow, and ice).

2. Ask the children to suggest what articles of clothing and equipment are necessary for us to stay warm, dry, healthy, and safe.

3. Let the children dress up the felt figure in appropriate winter garments.

4. Talk about the use of snow plows and rock salt to increase traction and melt snow so that cars and trucks can travel more easily. Show pictures of people and cars in the snow.

Variations/Ways to Extend:

- Read *City in the Winter* by Eleanor Schick (New York: Macmillan, 1970) and *The Winter Bear* by Ruth Craft (New York: Atheneum, 1975).
- Vary the activity to suit your geographic locale.

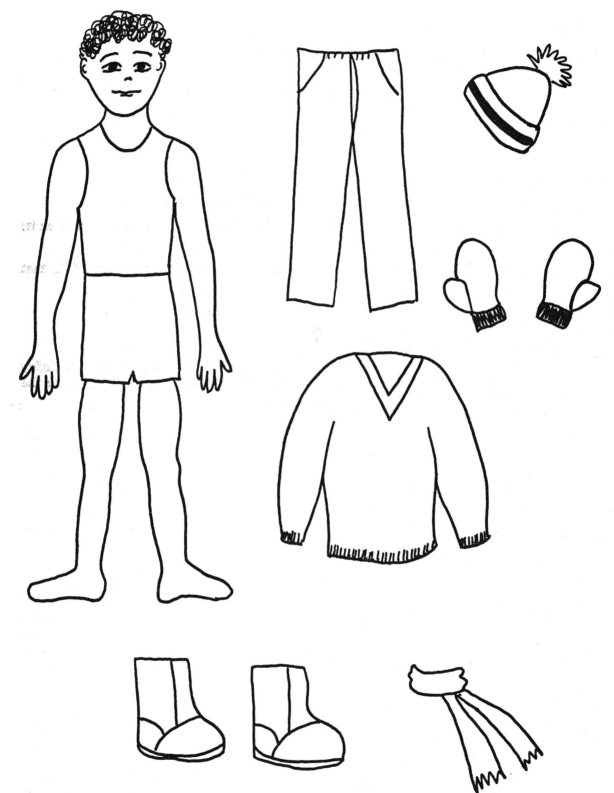

II-84 EXERCISE FOR FUN

Subject Area: Gross Motor Games

Concepts/Skills: Rolls a large ball to a target
Catches a large ball
Throws a ball

Objective: The children will engage in gross motor activities for fun and exercise.

Materials:
- Large ball
- Large basket

Procedure:

1. Warm up with a few minutes of "Simon Says" or "Hokey Pokey."

2. While standing, have each child take a turn rolling a large ball into a basket turned on its side.

3. Next, play "Name Ball." Say, "I throw the ball to (*name*)." As you name each child, that child tries to catch the ball. Ask the child to roll or throw it back to you.

4. Continue the game until all children have had at least one turn.

Variation/Way to Extend:

- Listen to Hap Palmer's album *Learning Basic Skills Through Music· Health and Safety* (available from Educational Activities, Inc., Freeport, NY 11520). Especially good are the songs "Posture Exercises" and "Exercise Every Day."

II–85 SAFETY RULES

Subject Area: Social Studies

Concept/Skill: Begins to understand the difference between safe and unsafe environments

Objectives: The children will discuss dangerous situations and help create safety rules.

Materials:
- Chart paper
- Marker

Procedure:

1. Write an experience chart from the ideas that the children dictate during this activity. Explain that many rules are made to keep people free from harm. Talk about what rules are necessary at school and why.

2. Allow the children to discuss various situations and come up with simple ideas that are safety rules. For example, if a situation is that people fall over misplaced toys, the rule might be: *Keep room neat.* Or, if the situation is that sharp objects can cut, the rule would be: *Do not play with knives and scissors.*

Variation/Way to Extend:

- Read the Caldecott Medal book *White Snow, Bright Snow* by Alvin R. Tresselt (New York: Lothrop, 1947).

II-86 I'M A LITTLE SNOWMAN

Subject Area: Language Arts

Concepts/Skills: Repeats a fingerplay
Imitates actions of teacher

Objective: The children will demonstrate the actions of a fingerplay about a snowman.

Material: • Words to the fingerplay

Procedure:

1. Teach the children the following fingerplay, sung to the tune of "I'm a Little Teapot":

> I'm a little snowman (*form circle in front of stomach with arms*)
> Round and fat,
> There are my buttons, (*point to pretend shirt buttons*)
> There is my hat. (*pat top of head*)
> When the hot sun comes out (*form circle above head with arms*)
> I can't play. (*shake head "no"*)
> Slowly, I just melt away. (*fall slowly to floor*)

2. Repeat the fingerplay several times with the children.

Variations/Ways to Extend:

- Listen to a recording of and sing "Frosty the Snowman."
- Show pictures of snowmen and snow scenes.
- Encourage the children to create snow figures out of flour dough.

II–87   TREATED AND UNTREATED SNOW

Subject Area: Science

Concepts/Skills: Observes objects closely
Compares rates of melting
Experiments

Objective: The children will observe snow melting with and without the addition of salt.

Materials:
- 2 glass jars with lids
- Snow
- Salt
- Pictures
- Timer or hourglass

Procedure:

1. Discuss how snow can become icy and slippery when it is packed down. Explain that that is why people wear boots and why cars use snow tires or chains. Also explain how salt is used on streets and walkways to melt the snow and make it safer on which to walk.

2. When it is a snowy day, fill two glass jars with snow. Sprinkle one with salt and put a picture of a salt shaker on the lid. Leave the other jar of snow untreated.

3. Ask the children to observe and compare the difference in the rates of melting. Keep track of time with a timer or hourglass.

Variation/Way to Extend:

- Read *The Big Snow* by Berta and Elmer Hader (New York: Macmillan, 1972).

II-88 APRICOT SNOWBALLS

Subject Area: Nutrition and Food Experience

Concepts/Skills: Follows directions
Participates in a group
Makes balls with dough

Objectives: The children will assist in pouring, mixing, stirring, and shaping a fruit ball for a snack.

Materials:
- 1½ cups dried apricots
- 2 cups shredded coconut
- ¾ cup sweetened condensed milk
- ¾ cup confectioners' sugar
- Measuring cup
- Bowl
- Blender (optional)
- Knife
- Wax paper

Procedure:

1. Let the children watch you chop dried apricots to a fine state or grind in a blender.

2. Place the ground apricots in a mixing bowl and let the children measure and add the coconut. Have one child stir this together. Let another child stir in the condensed milk.

3. Lay out a sheet of wax paper and pour the confectioners' sugar onto it.

4. Let each child shape a small amount of the apricot mixture into little balls and then roll them in the sugar.

5. Let these stand until firm, about half an hour. Then enjoy these apricot snowballs for a snack with a beverage.

Variations/Ways to Extend:

- Read *Snow is Falling* by Franklyn M. Branley (New York: Harper and Row, 1963).
- Obtain an 11″ × 14″ art reproduction of "Snow in New York" (#1342) by Robert Henri from the National Gallery of Art, Publications Service, Washington, DC 20565. Be sure to write for a catalog and prices.

II-89   SOAPFLAKE SNOWMAN

Subject Area: Art

Concepts/Skills: Pastes with one finger
Paints with a large brush or small sponge
Explores new materials and texture

Objective: The children will create a snowlike design from soapflakes.

Materials:
- Pre-cut snowman on white paper for each child
- Blue and black construction paper
- Pre-cut facial features and top hats
- Paste
- Brushes
- Small sponges
- ½ cup warm water
- ½ cup soapflakes

Procedure:

1. Give a pre-cut snowman shape to each child. Describe how the shape will be covered and textured with whipped soapflakes.

2. Prepare the soapflake mixture by mixing warm water with the soapflakes to form a thick paint.

3. Help the children apply the soapflake mixture to the snowman shape with either their hands, a large brush, or a small sponge.

4. Once the snowmen are dry, ask the children to paste them onto blue or black construction paper. Then have each child paste on eyes, a nose, a mouth, and a big hat.

Variation/Way to Extend:

- Read *The Snowman* by Raymond Briggs (New York: Random, 1978).

II–90 NUMBER IGLOO

Subject Area: Math

Concepts/Skills: Rote counts
Understands number concepts
Pastes with a finger or brush

Objectives: The children will construct an igloo and count the ice blocks used to make it.

Materials:
- Pre-cut igloo shape for each child
- White paper rectangles
- Blue paper
- Paste
- Photographs
- Poster paints
- Brushes

Procedure:

1. Show photographs of igloos, polar regions, and Eskimo people. Talk about how igloos are homes for people who live where it is very cold and snowy. Explain how ice blocks are piled on top of one another to make an igloo.

2. Give each child a pre-cut igloo shape. Let the children paste these onto blue paper.

3. Next, give each child six white rectangles and tell the children to count them. Ask the children to paste each rectangle onto the igloo shape, counting as they do so, and then recount the rectangles on the completed igloo.

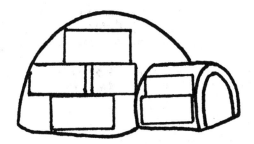

4. Have the children use poster paints to finish the picture by adding a sun, making it snow, showing an Eskimo person, or whatever the children decide.

Variations/Ways to Extend:

- Read *Snowman's Secret* by Robert Barry (New York: Macmillan, 1975).
- Extend this idea to the room's block corner. Ask the children to build igloos and other types of houses using the blocks available.

II-91 INVESTIGATING WATER

Subject Area: Science

Concepts/Skills: Observes objects closely
Understands sentences and questions as indicated by relevant answers
Understands that water has weight

Objectives: The children will explore and make generalizations about the properties of water.

Materials:
- Water
- Watch
- Tape
- Sponges
- Cleaner
- Stove
- Flour
- Pots
- Ice cube tray
- Large plastic tub

- Funnels
- Siphons
- Cups
- Clips
- Eggbeater
- Dishwashing liquid
- Rocks
- Paper
- Doll clothes

Procedure:

1. Ask a host of questions about water and let the children experiment to find the answers: "What does water feel like?" "Is it rough or smooth?" "Is it cold or hot?" "Is it wet or dry?"

2. Show that water evaporates by leaving a jar of water, with its volume marked, in a sunny place for a few days.

3. Explain that water cleans things, can be in different forms, and has many uses. Show water as a liquid, boiled to steam for a gas, and frozen to ice as a solid. (**Caution:** Be sure that the children stay away from the heat source when you boil the water.)

4. Prepare the children for water play by letting them siphon, pour, and funnel water and beat, float, and sink objects in a large plastic tub.

5. Mix some dishwashing liquid with water and blow bubbles.

6. Wash doll clothes and hang them to dry.

7. Water plants, clean the room, and make dough from flour and water. Use your imagination in using some of the other materials listed as you and the children explore the properties of water.

Variation/Way to Extend:

- Read *Floating & Sinking* by Franklyn M. Branley (New York: Harper and Row, 1967).

II-92 JACK AND JILL

Subject Area: Language Arts

Concepts/Skills: Repeats a simple rhyme or fingerplay
Uses past tense

Objective: The children will dramatize the words to a nursery rhyme.

Material: • Words to the rhyme

Procedure:

1. Explain some of the difficult vocabulary (*fetch, crown, caper*) the children will encounter in the nursery rhyme.

2. Teach the children the actions to go along with the following rhyme:

> Jack and Jill went up the hill (*wiggle two thumbs*)
>   To fetch a pail of water;
> Jack fell down and broke his crown, (*drop one thumb into lap*)
>   And Jill came tumbling after. (*drop other thumb into lap*)
> Then up got Jack and home did trot (*wiggle thumb up high*)
>   As fast as he could caper.
> And went to bed to mend his head (*rub thumb on hand*)
>   With vinegar and brown paper.

Variation/Way to Extend:

• Let the children experience that a bucket of water can be heavy. Have each child hold an empty bucket as you slowly fill it with water until it is too heavy to hold.

II-93 WATERCOLORS

Subject Area: Art

Concepts/Skills: Explores new materials
Paints with a brush

Objective: The children will observe the effect of water in bringing out a design on paper.

Materials:
- White paper
- White crayons
- Brushes
- Bowls of water
- Tubes of watercolors
- Sponges, paper toweling, blotters, rags, and similar items

Procedure:

1. Let the children experiment with materials that soak up water. Explain that during this activity, they will see how their papers soak up water and let a design show through.

2. Distribute white paper and white crayons. Ask the children to make any kind of design or picture they want on their papers using only the white crayons.

3. Now distribute bowls of water, slightly tinted with watercolors, and brushes. Let the children paint over the entire surface of their pictures.

4. Have the children notice that their crayon designs now appear. Tell them that this type of picture is known as a crayon resist.

Variation/Way to Extend:

- Provide the children with different-sized milk cartons, cut open at the top. Using small plastic containers, assist the children in filling the small containers with water and pouring the water into the milk cartons. Ask the children to count how many small containers of water fill up each milk carton.

II-94   ORANGE-BANANA SHAKE

Subject Area: Nutrition and Food Experience

Concepts/Skills: Develops fine motor movements of measuring and pouring
Observes changing states of liquid

Objective: The children will enjoy a beverage that includes the use of ice and water.

Materials: (This recipe makes about eight small servings)
- Blender
- Ice cubes
- 4 sliced bananas
- ½ cup frozen orange juice (still in solid form)
- ¼ teaspoon vanilla
- 4 cups reconstituted nonfat dry milk (still in powder form)
- Water
- Cups

Procedure:

1. To have the children experience firsthand how water changes things, reconstitute frozen orange juice with water and reconstitute nonfat dry milk powder with water. Have the children observe the results. Say, "This is milk made into a powder. All of its water has been taken out. We're going to put water back in again. Let's watch what happens!"

2. Pour the liquid orange juice and milk into the blender. Add the bananas, vanilla, and a few ice cubes and blend until a frothy drink is made.

3. Pour the orange-banana shake into individual cups for the children to enjoy at snack time.

Variation/Way to Extend:

- Read *The Man Who Didn't Wash His Dishes* by Phyllis Krasilovsky (New York: Doubleday, 1950).

Weekly Subtheme: Water and Ice

II-95 SNOWMAN TOSS

Subject Area: Gross Motor Games

Concept/Skill: Throws a beanbag at a target five feet away

Objective: The children will demonstrate throwing a beanbag into a snowman target.

Materials:
- 3 pre-cut large white paper circles
- Pre-cut black paper facial features, hat, buttons, and boots
- Tape
- Beanbag
- Paste
- Large sheet of oaktag
- Pictures or drawings of winter items

Procedure:

1. Lay three large white circles on the floor, side by side.

2. Tape the hat, facial features, buttons, and boots in place.

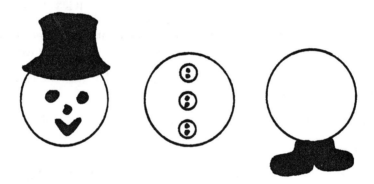

3. Ask the children to stand about five feet away from the three circles and try to throw a beanbag so that it lands in one of the circles. As the children progress, have them try to hit specific targets, such as the eyes, nose, or mouth.

4. After the game, let the children align the circles to make a snowman and paste the snowman on a large sheet of contrasting oaktag. Add cut-out pictures or drawings of winter items and display on a wall or bulletin board as a winter poster.

Variation/Way to Extend:

- Listen to Hap Palmer's album *Learning Basic Skills Through Music: Volume II* (available from Educational Activities, Inc., Freeport, NY 11520). Especially good are the songs "One Shape, Three Shapes" and "Triangle, Circle or Square."

TRANSPORTATION

- ○ By Land
- ○ By Rail
- ○ By Water
- ○ By Air

   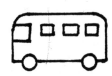

Weekly Subtheme: By Land

II-96 GETTING AROUND

Subject Area: Social Studies and Art

Concepts/Skills: Follows directions
Develops fine motor movements of cutting and pasting
Explores new materials

Objectives: The children will discuss methods of land transportation and construct a collage.

Materials:
- Pictures
- Scissors
- Magazines
- Paper
- Paste
- Buttons
- Macaroni wheels

Procedure:

1. Begin a discussion with the children about some of the types of land vehicles and methods of getting around they may have seen. Show pictures of cars, trucks, buses, bicycles, skates, motorcycles, and feet.

2. Then ask if they can think of unusual ways of moving about. Show pictures of skis, wagons, unicycles, carts, horses, donkeys, elephants, camels, and anything else you can think of.

3. Now concentrate on the car. Ask the children to cut pictures of cars from magazines and make a collage of these. For fun, tell them they can glue buttons or macaroni wheels onto the wheels in the pictures.

Variations/Ways to Extend:

- Read *Davy Goes Places* by Lois Lenski (New York: Walck, 1961).
- Using big buttons or macaroni wheels, let the children use these as wheels and draw or paint cars, trucks, motorcycles, carts, wagons, buses, or bicycles around them. Display the pictures on a wall at the children's eye level.

II-97   OUR CAR

Subject Area: Creative Dramatics and Movement

Concepts/Skills: Cooperates in a group
Plays using symbols

Objective: The children will enact a transportation idea aided by an arrangement of chairs and props.

Materials:
- Room chairs
- Props
- Basic ideas

Procedure:

1. Arrange two rows of three chairs, one behind the other, to make a car or a taxi. This allows six children at a time to pretend that they are in a vehicle. Add props to extend the play. These props might include real keys on a ring, a steering wheel, a stop sign, and a box for a tunnel or bridge.

2. Present the children with a basic idea and let them expand upon it. For example, say, "You are traveling by car through a crowded city, looking for a park. How do you find it?" Or, "You are a family out for a drive. Where will you stop for a picnic?"

Variation/Way to Extend:

- Listen to the "Car Song" from *Songs to Grow On* by Woody Guthrie (Folkways Records, 43 West 61 Street, New York, NY 10023).

II-98 ONE, TWO, THREE, FOUR WHEELS

Subject Area: Math

Concepts/Skills: Matches sets containing up to four objects
Develops fine motor movement of pasting

Objective: The children will complete a chart to match numbers of wheels to vehicles.

Materials: • Chart for each child
• Paper wheels
• Paste

Procedure:

1. Give each child a piece of construction paper with a simple chart drawn on it. In a vertical column, show a unicycle, a bicycle, a tricycle, and a car.

2. Talk about how each vehicle has one more wheel than the last—that is, one, two, three, and four.

3. Distribute the paper circles. Ask the children to match sets by recognizing how many wheels they see on each vehicle and pasting the same number of paper wheels next to each one.

Variation/Way to Extend:

• Read *The Little Auto* by Lois Lenski (New York: McKay, 1942).

II-99   LET'S SING

Subject Area: Music

Concepts/Skills: Performs with others
Participates in a song
Creates appropriate movements and lyrics

Objectives: The children will create lyrics having to do with transportation using a familiar tune.

Material: • Tune of the song

Procedure:

1. Have the children create lyrics for the familiar tune of "This Is the Way ..." For example:

   This is the way we ride in the car, ride in the car,
   ride in the car. This is the way we ride in the
   car, on the way to school.
   This is the way we ride a bicycle ...
   This is the way we pull a wagon ...
   This is the way we ride in a bus ...
   This is the way we ride a horse ...

2. Continue for many other types of land vehicles and methods of transportation discussed this week.

3. Ask the children to make the appropriate movements while they sing each line.

Variation/Way to Extend:

• Read *Big Red Bus* by Ethel and Leonard Kessler (New York: Doubleday, 1964).

II–100 MY RED WAGON

Subject Area: Art

Concept/Skill: Explores new materials

Objectives: The children will paint paper wagons, attach wheels, and discuss the parts.

Materials:
- Easel paper
- Red paint
- Yellow or white paint
- Sponges
- Black paper circles
- Paper fasteners
- Brushes

Procedure:

1. Give each child a sheet of easel paper with a large wagon shape drawn on it.

2. Ask the children to sponge-paint the wagons with red paint.

3. After the paintings have dried, give each child two black circles and gold **paper fasteners.** Help the children fasten these in place.

4. Talk about the parts of a wagon, the wheels, the steering mechanism, how to stop, **and so** on.

5. Help each child print his or her name in yellow or white paint on the side of the wagon.

Variations/Ways to Extend:

- Read *The Giant Nursery Book of Things That Go* by George Zaffo (New York: Doubleday, 1969).
- Let each child paint a small racing car in the manner described here and then choose **his or** her own number to paint on the side.

II–101   WHAT MADE THAT SOUND?

Subject Area: Language Arts

Concepts/Skills: Listens carefully
Identifies common sounds

Objective: The children will identify the sources of sounds recorded on a train trip.

Materials: • Audio tape made from real or recorded train sounds
• Tape player

Procedure:

1.   Create a tape from sounds you recorded during a subway or railroad expedition. If this cannot be done, listen to *A Train for Tommy,* a cassette recording with accompanying book available from A.A. Records, Inc., 1105 Globe Avenue, Mountainside, NJ 07092.

2.   Play one sound at a time for the children and have them try to identify the source of the sound. Some sounds to listen for are: the chug-chug of the train, the whistle blowing, a bell clamoring, the screech of the wheels on the track, the conductor yelling "All aboard," the slow starting-up sound, the doors opening and closing on a subway, and people getting on and off.

Variation/Way to Extend:

• Help the children make a recording of "Our Day at School." Play the tape periodically throughout the year for the children's identification of sounds.

Weekly Subtheme: By Rail

II–102   SHAPE TRAIN

Subject Area: Math

Concepts/Skills: Matches shapes
Points to and label shapes
Places objects on their outlines
Develops fine motor movement of pasting

Objective: The children will use a paper train to develop three shape skills.

Materials: • Large sheet of oaktag for each child
• Markers
• Scissors
• Colored paper
• Paste

Procedure:

1. Draw a train on oaktag for each child. Draw an engine and four rectangles representing cars. In the center of each car, draw a different shape (circle, square, triangle, and rectangle).

2. Cut a number of matching shapes from colored paper.

3. As the children handle these shapes, encourage them to point to which is the square, the circle, the triangle, and the rectangle. Ask them to name each shape.

4. Have the children paste the appropriate paper shape onto each shape outline in the cars of their individual trains.

Variations/Ways to Extend:

• Try this activity using a circus train or a camel train.
• Read *Choo, Choo* by Virginia L. Burton (Boston: Houghton Mifflin, 1937).

II–103   BE A TRAIN

Subject Area: Creative Dramatics and Movement

Concepts/Skills: Cooperates in a group
Follows directions
Dramatizes a simple story
Understands opposites

Objective: The children will apply various human character traits to their playful portrayal of a train.

Materials: • Book
• Pictures

Procedure:

1. Read a book about trains. One good example is *The Little Engine That Could* by Watty Piper (Cutchogue, NY: Buccaneer Books, 1981, repr.).

2. Discuss with the children the many types of trains, such as passenger, freight, subway, and monorail. Have plenty of pictures on hand to show them. Talk about the different jobs the different types of trains do and ways that the rails are constructed or positioned. Tell the children that the locomotive is the first car on the train and the caboose is the last.

3. Encourage a relaxed, playful atmosphere and allow the children to pretend to be trains. Give directions to their play with statements in which you assign roles ("Be the caboose"), describe the action ("Be a tired old train going uphill"), or set up a situation ("Be a shiny new monorail talking to an old steam locomotive"). Some of these directives could be to individuals or to small groups or to the whole group. Many directives can also be given. For example, "Be a train moving slowly, now more quickly, now fast." "Be a tall train, a short train, a small train, a big train." "Be a proud train, an angry train, a happy train, a sad train."

Variation/Way to Extend:

• Encourage the children's continued train-play without your directives. Bring in a toy railroad, lantern, hat, signs, and other train-related items to further encourage the children's play.

II–104   GET ON BOARD

Subject Area: Music

Concepts/Skills: Memorizes and repeats a simple song
Participates with pleasure

Objective: The children will learn a new song about "boarding" a train.

Materials: • Words to the song
• Chairs
• Whistle

Procedure:

1. Teach the children the words and tune to this popular folk song:

    Get on board lit-tle chil-dren,
    Get on board lit-tle chil-dren,
    Get on board lit-tle chil-dren,
    There's room for many and more.

2. Use the children's names in the song. For example, "Get on board lit-tle Tim-my."

3. Once the children have learned the song, line up the room's chairs into a train and have the children sing while "on board." Let one child blow a whistle to start and have the children move their arms in circles bent at the elbow to simulate train wheels.

Variations/Ways to Extend:

• Take a train excursion as a class or visit a train station. Another trip idea is to visit the home of a model train enthusiast in your area.
• Play a recording of "Little Train" from the *Once Upon a Time Suite* by Donaldson.

II-105 BOX CARS

Subject Areas: Art and Social Studies

Concepts/Skills: Explores
Paints with a large brush

Objective: The children will construct a train from cardboard boxes.

Materials:
- Several large cardboard boxes
- Paints
- Brushes
- Cardboard circles
- Paper fasteners
- Cord
- Razor

Procedure:

1. Cut off the tops and the bottoms of several large cardboard boxes.

2. Have the children paint them different colors to represent the various cars of a train. For example, the engine could be painted silver, the coal car could be painted black, and the caboose, red.

3. Attach cardboard circles with large paper fasteners to serve as wheels.

4. Use lengths of cord to attach each car to the one behind it.

5. Ask a child to step inside a box and pull it up around his or her waist. Then have several other children do this with the other boxes to form a "train."

6. Ask the "train" to walk around the room, tooting and whistling.

Variations/Ways to Extend:

- Read *Two Little Trains* by Margaret W. Brown (Reading, MA: Addison-Wesley, 1949).
- Create a railroad track with strips of masking tape for the children to use as a guide as they move around the room in their cardboard box train.

II–106   OUR SAILBOATS

Subject Area: Science

Concepts/Skills: Observes
Experiments

Objectives: The children will construct sailboats and test them in water.

Materials:
- Styrofoam blocks or flower-arrangement bases
- Popsicle sticks
- White paper squares
- Hole puncher
- Tape
- Large tub of water
- Marker

Procedure:

1. Explain to the children that when air outdoors moves around, it is called wind. Have the children blow on their hands and wave their arms around to feel the air that is moving and making a small wind. Tell them that a sailboat moves because wind blows into its sails and pushes the boat along.

2. Prepare the white squares for use as sails by punching one hole near the top and one hole near the bottom of the paper.

3. Help the children insert the tongue depressors into the sails and tape them in place. Tell the children that this is the mast with the sail.

4. Label each sail with the child's name.

5. Insert the mast and sail into the block or base and allow the children to sail their boats in a large tub of water.

Variations/Ways to Extend:
- Vary the size and the position of the sails to see if there is any effect on speed or balance.
- Read *The Little Sailboat* by Lois Lenski (New York: Walck, 1937).
- Obtain an 11″ × 14″ art reproduction of "Felucca Off Gibraltar" (#2352) by Thomas Chambers from the National Gallery of Art, Publications Service, Washington, DC 20565. Be sure to write for a catalog and prices.

II-107   WHERE DO THE BOATS GO?

Subject Area: Language Arts

Concepts/Skills: Listens to a simple poem
Comprehends

Objectives: The children will listen to and enjoy a wonderful poem about boats.

Material: • Words to "Where Go the Boats" by Robert Louis Stevenson

Procedure:

1. Establish a relaxed atmosphere for poetry reading. Read the poem **expressively to the children.** Ask them to make pictures in their minds of the words as you read **the poem again.**

WHERE GO THE BOATS?

Dark brown is the river,
  Golden is the sand.
It flows along forever,
  With trees on either hand.

Green leaves a-floating,
  Castles of the foam,
Boats of mine a-boating—
  Where will all come home?

On goes the river
  And out past the mill,
Away down the valley,
  Away down the hill.

Away down the river,
  A hundred miles or more,
Other little children
  Shall bring my boats ashore.

2. Ask the children some questions about the poem after the second **reading simply to be certain** that they understood that the poem is about boats and a river. Ask, "What other images were you able to make in your minds?"

Variation/Way to Extend:

• Use the poem as a stimulus for a painting in which the colors mentioned (**dark brown,** golden, green) are used.

II-108   PINK BOAT, BLUE BOAT

Subject Area: Math

Concepts/Skills: Sorts objects into two given categories
Develops visual discrimination

Objective: The children will sort boat shapes into two categories.

Materials:
- Blue index cards
- Pink index cards
- Scissors
- Marker
- Two shirt boxes
- Blue paper

Procedure:

1. From a stack of blue index cards, cut out the shape of a sailboat. Fill in the details with a marker.

2. From a stack of pink index cards, cut out the shape of a tugboat. Fill in the details with a marker.

3. Do this activity with individual children or with a small group. Just be sure to prepare enough cards for each child to have five of each type with which to work.

4. Line two shirt boxes with blue paper (pretending they are lakes) as containers for sorting.

5. Draw the outline of the sailboat on one "lake" and the tugboat on the other.

6. Ask the children to sort the boats by shape into the two lakes.

Variation/Way to Extend:

- Use the boats to facilitate other sorting activities. You might, for example, line up three sailboats and insert a tugboat in between two. Ask, "Which is different and does not belong?"

II–109   ROW THE BOAT

Subject Area: Music

Concepts/Skills: Responds to rhythm
Memorizes and repeats a simple song

Objective: The children will sing a song about being in a rowboat.

Materials:
- Words to "Row, Row, Row Your Boat"
- Sea captain's and sailor's hats
- Oars (brooms or made from cardboard)
- Pictures
- Recording

Procedure:

1. Show pictures of rowboats and discuss the idea of a rowboat with the children. Explain how it is small and moves through the water powered only by a person or persons pulling on a pair of oars.

2. Have the children sing "Row, Row, Row Your Boat" while sitting cross-legged on the floor, in pairs, and facing each other.

3. Use whatever props you can (hats, cardboard oars) to enhance the mood created of being in a boat. Tell the children to move and sway to the rhythm of the music. (If you would like to have the children sing along to a recording of the song, obtain a copy of the album *Rhythms of Childhood* by Ella Jenkins, available from Scholastic Records.)

Variation/Way to Extend:

- Explain to the children that people often fish from rowboats. Make fishing poles from new pencils (no points) with string tied to one end and magnets attached to the other end of the string. Make paper fish with a paper clip fastened on as a mouth. Have the children fish for these from their boat positions. If possible, allow them to take their "fishing pole" and "fish" home so they may experiment more with magnetism.

II–110 LACE BOATS

Subject Area: Art

Concept/Skill: Laces following a sequence of holes

Objective: The children will construct paper boats using a lacing technique.

Materials: • Colored tagboard or lightweight posterboard
• Hole puncher
• Tissues
• Scissors
• Yarn
• Tape

Procedure:

1. From large sheets of tagboard or posterboard, cut out boat shapes that are approximately 9″ × 12″. Cut enough shapes so that each child will have two.

2. Punch holes along the inside edge of the boat shapes, all the way around.

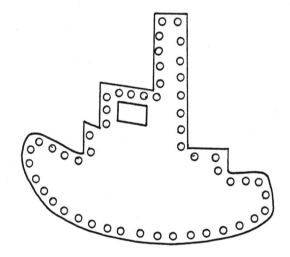

3. Give each child a length of yarn with one end wrapped with tape and the other end knotted.

4. Show each child how to go through a hole, over the edge of the paper, and through the next hole. Be sure that the two shapes are being laced together.

5. Have the children continue until three-fourths of the boat is laced. Then have each child gently stuff the boat with tissues.

6. Help the children to finish the lacing and let them take their stuffed boats home.

Variations/Ways to Extend:

• For a more individualized boat, have the children decorate their boat shapes with felt pens or crayons before lacing.
• Read *Pop-Up Boats* by Albert G. Miller (New York: Random House, 1966).

II–111   UP OR DOWN?

Subject Area: Math

Concept/Skill: Sorts objects into two categories

Objective: The children will sort pictures of objects into two categories.

Materials:
- Pictures
- Magazine pictures
- Paste
- Construction paper
- Scissors

Procedure:

1. Discuss air transportation with the children. Ask, "Who has been on a plane?" "What was it like?" "Was it fun?" "Why?" "Why not?" Talk about airplanes carrying people and things through the sky. Show pictures of airplanes. Talk about other types of air vehicles, too, such as helicopters, seaplanes, gliders, rockets, hot air balloons, and blimps.

2. Cut and mount an assortment of magazine pictures of various means of transportation. Include examples of the other types of transportation (cars, buses, trains, and boats) previously discussed.

3. Ask the children to sort the mounted pictures according to those that go in the air and those that do not.

Variation/Way to Extend:

- Read *Journey to the Moon* by Erich Fuchs (New York: Delacorte, 1970).

Weekly Subtheme: By Air

II–112 I'M AN AIRPLANE

Subject Area: Language Arts

Concepts/Skills: Memorizes and repeats a simple fingerplay
Moves body in response to simple teacher commands

Objectives: The children will listen to and act out a fingerplay about an airplane.

Material: • Words to the fingerplay

Procedure:

1. Teach the children the following fingerplay and accompanying motions:

> I'm a happy airplane. (*spread arms wide*)
> I fly through the sky. (*pretend to fly*)
> I swoop down low, (*bend low as you walk or run*)
> Then I fly up so high. (*stand tall as you walk or run*)
> My wing dips to the left, (*lean to the left*)
> My wing dips to the right, (*lean to the right*)
> And then I fly away (*straighten arms and run*)
> Far out of sight. (*"fly" across the room*)

2. Repeat the fingerplay several times with the children.

Variations/Ways to Extend:

- Give the children paper streamers to use as they act out this fingerplay to heighten their sense of air and movement.
- Arrange for a pilot to visit the class and talk about his or her job.

II–113   AIRPLANE COOKIES

Subject Area: Nutrition and Food Experience

Concept/Skill: Develops fine motor movements of making balls and snakes with dough

Objective: The children will shape airplanes from cookie dough.

Materials:
- Cookie dough
- Cookie sheets
- Oven
- Tongue depressor

Procedure:

1. Prepare the cookie dough according to the package's directions.

2. Give each child two small handfuls of dough. Encourage them to roll the dough into balls and then make snake shapes.

3. Show the children how to crisscross the long shapes to form the body, wings, and tail of an airplane.

4. Use the end of a tongue depressor to press each child's initials into the plane.

5. Bake and eat the airplanes when done. (**Caution:** Be sure the children stay away from the heat.)

Variation/Way to Extend:

- Use clay instead of cookie dough and paint the airplanes when the clay is dry. Let the children take their planes home.

II–114   JUMPING ON THE MOON

Subject Area: Gross Motor Game

Concepts/Skills: Jumps with both feet
Jumps over a barrier
Plays using symbols

Objectives: The children will practice jumping skills and think about airplanes.

Materials: • Large open area
• Small blocks

Procedure:

1. Tell the children that they are going to pretend being parachute jumpers, jumping out of airplanes.

2. Ask them to jump with two feet and land on two feet while keeping their balance.

3. Now have them pretend they are on the moon. Have them jump over large "boulders" (small blocks) that are in their way. Be sure the children jump with both feet and land on two feet.

Variation/Way to Extend:

• Do this activity while reciting the nursery rhyme "Jack Be Nimble":

Jack be nimble,
Jack be quick,
Jack jump over
the candlestick

II-115   STRAW-PAINTED AIRPLANE

Subject Area: Art

Concepts/Skills: Explores new materials
Expresses self creatively

Objective: The children will straw-paint paper airplanes.

Materials: • Construction paper cut in an airplane shape (see the pattern on the next page)
• Spoons
• Straws
• Paints

Procedure:

1. First let the children become familiar with blowing through straws. Tell them to put their hand near the other end of the straw and feel the air coming out.

2. Give each child an airplane shape.

3. Help each child drop a small amount of paint from a spoon onto his or her paper plane.

4. Then have the children paint by blowing through the straw in all different directions.

5. Display the completed paintings when they are dry.

Variations/Ways to Extend:

• Read *The Little Airplane* by Lois Lenski (New York: McKay, 1938).
• If the children are preparing valentines this month, let them pretend that their cards are delivered by transport planes.

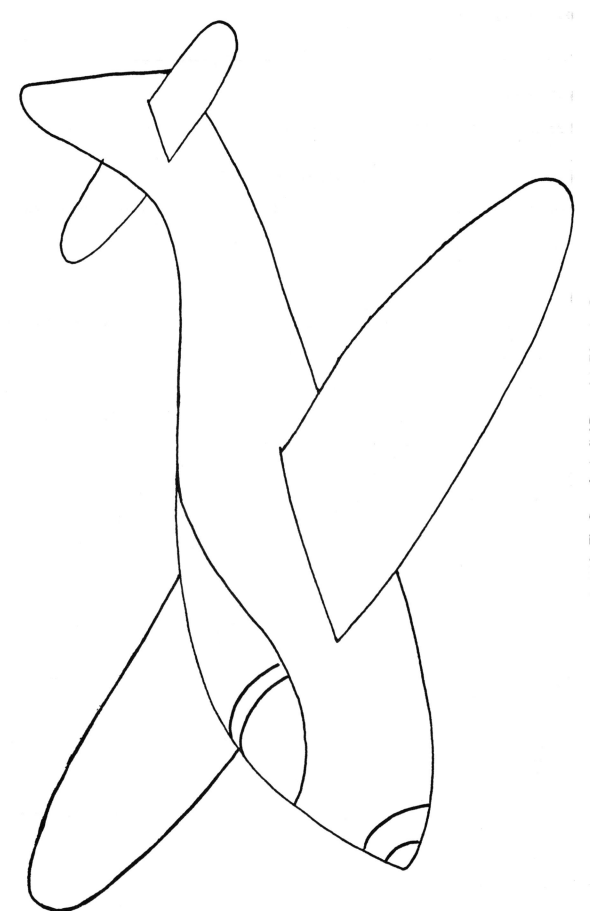

ANIMALS

- ○ Forest Animals
- ○ Pets
- ○ Zoo Animals
- ○ The Circus and Circus Animals

II–116 BIRD NESTS

Subject Area: Science

Concepts/Skills: Works with clay
Solves problems

Objectives: The children will collect natural materials to combine with clay and construct bird nests.

Materials:
- Twigs and dry leaves
- Feathers
- String
- Clay
- Paper bag for each child
- Actual bird nest (optional)

Procedure:

1. Discuss the many forest animals that exist and concentrate on those most familiar to the children, such as deer, rabbits, raccoons, squirrels, chipmunks, and birds. Ask, "In the woods, where do you think rabbits live?" (in low shrubs) "Where do you think squirrels live?" (in branch nests or tree hollows). Explain to the children that all animals need food, water, shelter for protection, and a place where they can take care of their young. Birds usually build nests for this purpose. Ask, "What do you think birds use to make their nests?" (often string, twigs, dry leaves, and feathers). If possible, show the children an actual bird nest. Be sure that this nest is not currently being used by any birds.
2. Give each child a paper bag and go on a walk to collect some nest-building materials.
3. After returning, give each child a portion of clay and have them round out a base for a nest. Like some birds, let the children add the other materials to the clay to build the nests. Remind the children that birds accomplish this tricky building without any fingers!
4. Let the children make some tiny eggs from play dough for each nest, too.

Variations/Ways to Extend:

- Invite a parent to bring in a bird for the children to observe. Or, visit a wildlife center in your area.
- Read *It's Nesting Time* by Roma Gans (New York: Thomas Y. Crowell, 1972).
- As background music this week, play some selections from *Carnival of the Animals* by Saint-Saëns (RCA Records).

II–117 ANIMAL RACES

Subject Area: Gross Motor Game

Concepts/Skills: Understands that animals move in different ways
Jumps three times with both feet
Walks on tiptoe
Crawls

Objectives: The children will imitate the movements of animals while engaging in physical games.

Material: • Large open area

Procedure:

1. Teach the children the following four games:

   Bear Race—Divide the class into two teams. Ask the children to get down on all fours and walk on their hands and feet. See which team can get all its members into the "woods" (goal line set opposite them) first.

   Bunny Race—Have the children jump three times with both feet at a time as they make their way across the room to a "bunny hole."

   Caterpillar Race—Have the children lie down and crawl along on their bellies, inching their way across to a "tree."

   Bird Race—Have the children "fly" on tiptoes for five steps at a time, flying across the room to their "nests."

2. Play these games throughout the week.

Variations/Ways to Extend:

- Embellish the games by giving the children some fabric scraps (fake fur, feathers) to wear.
- Set up an obstacle course of chairs and pretend that they are trees. Ask the little "animals" to scurry around in a certain order or touch each "tree" in a certain sequence.

II-118 STUFFED ANIMALS

Subject Area: Art

Concepts/Skills: Paints with a large brush
Develops fine motor movements of stuffing paper and pasting.

Objective: The children will construct three-dimensional animal shapes.

Materials
- Kraft paper
- Newspaper
- Stapler
- Paints
- Brushes
- Scissors
- Yarn, fabric scraps, fake fur, pipe cleaners
- Paste

Procedure:

1. Select a few of the animals discussed so far this week. For each child, cut out an animal shape from two pieces of kraft paper.
2. Staple the edges together three-fourths of the way around.

3. Ask the children to paint and decorate the animals with yarn, fabric scraps, and the other items you have collected.
4. Help the children stuff the animals with newspaper to form a solid shape.
5. Finish the animals by stapling the remaining edges.

Variations/Ways to Extend:

- At snack time, serve some nuts, berries, fruits, and vegetables that forest animals like to eat.
- Read *Animal Jackets* by Aileen Fisher (Los Angeles: Bowmar, 1973). A filmstrip and record or cassette are also available.

II–119 LET'S LOOK IN AND SEE

Subject Area: Music

Concepts/Skills: Repeats a simple song
Participates with enthusiasm

Objective: The children will participate in a song about animals.

Materials: • Words and music to "Let's Look In and See"

Procedure:

1. Explain to the children that this song will make them think about nature.
2. Ask the children to fill in the missing animals as they look into the "forests" and "seas" of their imagination.
3. Describe the motions to the song, which include cupping hands around the mouth when calling out the names of the animals and cupping hands around the eyes when looking.
4. Sing the song several times, letting individual children complete the song, too.

Variations/Ways to Extend:

• Ask the children to describe the characteristics of the animals they see.
• Read *Home for a Bunny* by Margaret W. Brown (Racine, WI: Western, 1983).

Let's Look in and See!

Words and Music by BOB MESSANO
Arranged by John Sheehan

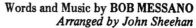

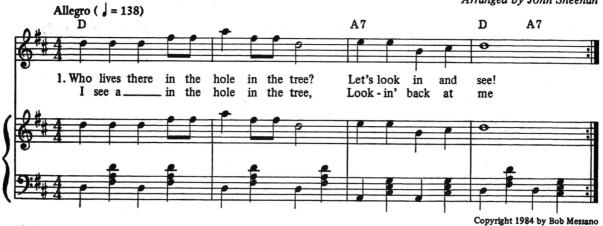

Allegro (♩ = 138)

1. Who lives there in the hole in the tree? Let's look in and see!
   I see a _____ in the hole in the tree, Look-in' back at me

2. Who lives down in a hole in the ground?
   Let's look in and see!
   I see a _____ in the hole in the ground,
   Lookin' back at me!

3. Who lives in the water of a bubbly stream?
   Let's look in and see!
   I see a _____ in the bubbly stream,
   Lookin' back at me!

4. Who lives at the bottom of the deep blue sea?
   Let's look in and see!
   I see a _____ in the deep blue sea,
   Lookin' back at me!

II–120   BABY ANIMALS

Subject Area: Thinking Games

Concepts/Skills: Pairs related pictures
Understands that there are many kinds of animals

Objectives: The children will use the wall display to practice matching and labeling animals.

Materials:
- Pictures of adult animals
- Pictures of baby animals
- Bulletin board space
- Yarn
- Tacks
- Tape
- Animal name labels

Procedure:

1. Divide the bulletin board space into two columns headed "Adult Animal" and "Baby Animal."
2. Arrange the pictures of the adult animals under the first column. Place each adult's name label next to the appropriate picture.
3. Arrange the baby animal pictures in the second column, but *do not* put them in the same order as the adults. Place each baby's name label next to the appropriate picture.
4. Attach a long piece of yarn to each picture in the adult animal column.
5. Ask the children to match the adult to the baby by bringing the yarn over and taping it in place. Here are some examples:

ADULT ANIMAL	BABY ANIMAL
deer	kit
fox	bunny
rabbit	fawn
raccoon	cub

Variations/Ways to Extend:

- Make another display of pictures for habitats. Here are some examples:

HABITAT	ANIMAL
tree hole	bird
sky	squirrel
forest	rabbit
underground burrow	deer

- Read *Play with Me* (New York: Penguin, 1976) and the Caldecott Honor Book *Just Me* (New York: Viking, 1965), both by Marie H. Ets.

II-121   PET DAY

Subject Area: Social Studies

Concepts/Skills: Engages in simple conversation
Uses pronouns (*I, he, she, you, me*) correctly
Asks questions

Objectives: The children will participate in discussions and make observations about pets.

Material: • Parents visiting with pets

Procedure:

1. In advance of this lesson, invite parents to bring in their families' pets. Schedule these visits at different times throughout the day.
2. Initiate a discussion with the children about common household pets—dogs, cats, birds, hamsters, guinea pigs, gerbils, fish, and turtles.
3. When the parents visit with the pets, invite the children to talk about their particular pets. Ask, "What is the pet's name?" "How is it cared for?" "What does it eat and how often?" "How old is the pet?" "What noise does it make?" "How does it get exercise?" "Where does it stay at your house?"
4. Let the children ask questions of the parent and child about their pet. Ask, "What is the best thing about your pet?" "What is not so good about having this kind of pet?"

Variations/Ways to Extend:

- When the children are using clay, encourage them to mold basic animal shapes and to sculpt their real or pretend pets.
- Let the children work with a Judy Puzzle about pets, such as "Fish." These puzzles are available from Judy Instructional Aids, The Judy Co., 250 James Street, Morristown, NJ 07960.

II-122   MOTHER CAT AND KITTENS

Subject Area: Gross Motor Games

Concepts/Skills: Understands that there are many kinds of animals
Identifies common sounds
Rote counts

Objective: The children will play a game demonstrating animal sounds and number awareness.

Material: • Large open area

Procedure:

1. Choose one child to be "Mother Cat." Choose four other children to be "Kittens."
2. Ask "Mother Cat" to pretend to sleep while the "Kittens" run and hide. When she awakens, "Mother Cat" asks, "Where are my kittens?" The kittens softly answer, "Meow, meow, meow." Tell "Mother Cat" to follow the sounds and bring her kittens back to the circle or original spot. "Mother Cat" then counts to see if she has all four kittens.
3. Repeat this game until all children who want to play have had a chance.

Variation/Way to Extend:

• Use other pet animals and animal sounds to play the game. For example, "Mother Dog" and "Puppies" would say "woof, woof," and "Father Bird" and "Chicks" would say "tweet-tweet."

II-123   TEXTURED ANIMALS

Subject Area: Art

Concepts/Skills: Understands that there are many kinds of animals
Develops fine motor movements of pasting and using scissors

Objective: The children will construct textured pictures of pet animals.

Materials: • Pre-cut animal shapes
• Construction paper
• Scissors
• Textured materials
• Glue

Procedure:

1.   Provide pre-cut paper shapes of common pets. Let each child select his or her own choice with which to work.

2.   Have the children paste the animal shapes onto construction paper.
3.   Provide textured materials for the children to use in covering the animals' bodies. These materials can include leather, tiny ceramic tiles, wallpaper, patterned cloth, textured fabric, cotton, yarn, rug scraps, fake fur, and feathers.
4.   Help the children cut these materials and paste them onto the animal shapes.

Variations/Ways to Extend:

• Research with the children appropriate foods for each animal. Cut out magazine pictures or use real samples for the children to paste onto their pictures near the animals' heads.
• Read the Caldecott Medal Book *Madeline's Rescue* by Ludwig Bemelmans (New York: Penguin, 1953).

II–124   ANIMAL COOKIES

Subject Area: Nutrition and Food Experience

Concepts/Skills: Develops fine motor movements of mixing, pouring, rolling, and cutting
Paints with a brush

Objectives: The children will create, decorate, bake, and eat animal-shaped cookies.

Materials:
- Basic butter cookie dough
- Animal cookie cutters
- Evaporated milk
- Cookie sheets
- Food coloring
- Brushes
- Oven

Procedure:

1. Use a standard butter cookie recipe to form the cookie dough.
2. Allow the children to roll and shape animals or roll and use animal cookie cutters to form animals.
3. Make "cookie paint" by mixing evaporated milk with a few drops of food coloring. With clean thin brushes, let the children paint their animals.
4. Bake according to the recipe's directions and enjoy as a snack. (**Caution:** Be sure the children stay away from the heat.)

Variations/Ways to Extend:

- Bake enough cookies so that the children can make pairs (twins) of cats, dogs, birds, and other animals.
- Tell the children the poem "Bird Talk" by Aileen Fisher. It is found in *Poems to Read to the Very Young*, compiled by Josette Frank (New York: Random House, 1982).
- Read *Angus Lost* by Margorie Flack (New York: Doubleday, 1941).

Weekly Subtheme: Pets

II–125   ANIMALS GO!

Subject Area: Creative Dramatics and Movement

Concepts/Skills: Understands that animals move in different ways
Develops gross motor movements of walking, jumping, stretching, running, and hopping

Objective: The children will imitate the movements of some common household pets.

Materials: • Large open area
• Background music

Procedure:

1. Play an instrumental recording as background music, such as *Afternoon of a Faun* by Debussy.
2. Discuss how different animals move and ask the children to "be the animal talked about." For example:

> cat—walks, climbs, stretches, jumps, rolls a ball
> dog—walks, runs, does tricks, sleeps on its side
> gerbil—climbs, jumps, leaps, runs, scampers
> hamster—runs, burrows, climbs, dives, goes up a ladder
> guinea pig—moves slowly, waddles, cuddles, drinks from a water dispenser
> parakeet—flies, hops, climbs, sleeps with head under a wing
> turtle—crawls, swims, climbs slowly, digs a hole
> fish—swims, stays still, darts away, jumps out of water

Variation/Way to Extend:

• Read the Caldecott winner *Frog Went A-Courtin'*, retold by John Langstaff and Feodor Rojankovsky (San Diego: Harcourt Brace Jovanovich, 1955).

II-126   TRIP TO THE ZOO

Subject Area: Social Studies

Concepts/Skills: Observes
Develops auditory memory
Understands that there are many kinds of animals

Objectives: The children will observe the animals at the zoo and later identify their sounds from a tape.

Materials: • Pictures
• Zoo visit
• Animal-shaped name tags
• Tape recorder

Procedure:

1. Arrange for a visit to a local zoo with the children. A children's petting zoo would be a wonderful concrete experience.
2. Have the children wear animal-shaped name tags when they visit the zoo.
3. Prepare the children for the zoo trip by discussing and showing pictures of some of the animals they might see, such as bears, elephants, giraffes, lions, monkeys, and zebras. Explain that a zoo is a safe way to see these animals.
4. Take along a tape recorder to the zoo and record as many animal sounds as you can.
5. Back in the classroom, use the tape to have the children recall which animals made the various sounds. Be sure to have a list handy of the animals in the order in which they were taped so that you can verify the children's guesses.

Variations/Ways to Extend:

• Have the children paint their impressions of the zoo trip.
• Teach the following fingerplay to the children:

> Two little monkeys (*bounce fingers on one another*)
> Bouncing on a bed,
> One fell off
> And bumped his head. (*hold head*)
> Mother called the doctor (*make dialing motions*)
> And the doctor said,
> No more monkeys (*shake finger*)
> Bouncing on the bed!

II-127   ANIMALS AT THE ZOO

Subject Area: Language Arts

Concept/Skill: Repeats a simple fingerplay

Objective: The children will demonstrate the actions in a fingerplay about the zoo.

Material: • Words to the fingerplay

Procedure:

1.   Teach the following fingerplay to the children:

> This is the way the elephant goes, (*clasp hands together, straighten arms and swing*)
> With a long trunk instead of a nose.
> The buffalo, all shaggy and fat, (*position pointer fingers on sides of forehead*)
> Has two sharp horns in place of a hat.
> The hippo with his mouth so wide, (*puts hands together at wrists and open and close*)
> Lets you see what is inside.
> The wiggly snake upon the ground, (*place hands together and weave back and forth*)
> Crawls so slow without a sound.
> But monkeys see and monkeys do, (*place thumb in ears and wiggle hands*)
> Are the funniest animals at the zoo!

2.   Let the children try to think of other zoo animals whose motions they can act out.

Variations/Ways to Extend:

- Ask the children to add bodily movements to dramatize the animals as they are mentioned in the fingerplay.
- Listen to "The Elephant" on Hap Palmer's album *Learning Basic Skills Through Music: Volume I* (available from Educational Activities, Inc., Freeport, NY 11520).
- Show pictures of the animals mentioned in the fingerplay and have the children respond with the appropriate movement.

Weekly Subtheme: Zoo Animals

II-128 COLOR BEARS

Subject Area: Math

Concepts/Skills: Matches shapes and colors
Matches sets containing up to five objects

Objective: The children will use bear-shaped cards for a classification activity.

Materials:
- Colored oaktag in six colors
- Cardboard bear (see pattern on next page)
- Pencil
- Scissors

Procedure:

1. Cut the bear pattern from a piece of cardboard. Use this as a template to trace the bear onto blue, yellow, red, green, orange, and purple oaktag. Make two of each color so that you'll have twelve cards.
2. With individual children or a small group, instruct them to observe the colored bears spread out on the table. Single out a red one. Ask, "What color is this bear?" Tell the child to point to another red bear and let the child put the two red bears together.
3. Repeat this with each of the other colors, mixing them all up again after each is singled out. Encourage the child to pair the bears again on his or her own.
4. Lay out a pattern that includes three bears of different colors. Ask the child to repeat the pattern shown. Try this using four different color bears and then five.

Variations/Ways to Extend:

- Use the bear cards for counting. Say, "Count out two bears." "Count out five bears."
- Use the cards to help the children practice using position words and colors. Say, "Put a yellow bear under (on top of, beside, next to) a green bear."

II–129 ANIMALS RUN HOME

Subject Area: Gross Motor Games

Concepts/Skills: Begins learning the "give and take" of play
Follows directions
Develops body coordination by running

Objective: The children will participate in a motor activity involving zoo animals.

Materials: • Large open area
• Animal stickers

Procedure:

1. Ask the children to form a circle.
2. Put a different animal sticker (bear, elephant, lion, camel) on each child's sleeve so that he or she can see it.
3. Select a "Caller" to call out two animal names. Those two children with the particular stickers must leave their "home" in the circle and change places. The "Caller" tries to get to one of their homes first. Whoever does not find a home becomes the next "Caller."

Variations/Ways to Extend:

• Listen to selections, such as "Going to the Zoo," from Hap Palmer's album *Folk Song Carnival* (available from Educational Activities, Inc., Freeport, NY 11520).
• Find out about animal homes in the book *Thackeray Turtle* by M. L. Leiss.

II–130   ELEPHANT FRIEND

Subject Area: Art

Concepts/Skills: Develops fine motor movement of pasting
Paints with a large brush

Objectives: The children will construct and decorate paper bag elephants.

Materials:
- Brown paper bags
- Newspapers
- Paints
- Brushes
- String
- Scissors
- Cardboard dowels
- Pre-cut triangles
- Pre-cut circles
- Pre-cut legs
- Pre-cut tails
- Paste

Procedure:

1. Have each child stuff a brown paper bag about halfway full with newspapers. Secure the bag at that point with a piece of string.
2. Insert a cardboard dowel into the remaining section of the bag and again secure with string.
3. Let the children paint the elephant bodies.
4. When the paint is dry, let the children paste on circle eyes, triangle ears, rectangle legs, and a curly tail cut from ribbon or crepe paper streamers.

Variation/Way to Extend:

- Let the children draw pictures of elephants or paint huge elephants at the easel. Cut out the elephants and display them in a line with the trunks holding tails, circus-style.

Weekly Subtheme: Circus and Circus Animals

II–131 CIRCUS STICK PUPPETS

Subject Area: Social Studies

Concepts/Skills: Engages in simple conversation
Holds crayon with fingers
Pastes

Objectives: The children will participate in a discussion about the circus and create stick puppets.

Materials:
- Paper animal shapes
- Paste
- Scissors
- Crayons
- Tongue depressors
- Paper fasteners
- Clown or makeup artist

Procedure:

1. Begin a discussion with the children about the circus. Invite a children's-party clown or a little-theater makeup artist to show how clown makeup is applied. Perhaps a few of the children would like to become clowns for a day!

2. Ask the children if they have ever seen the circus. Allow them to describe what they recall. Explain that many families work in a circus, with parents teaching their children how to perform wonderful acts. Mention that some of the animals usually found in the circus are elephants, bears, horses, lions, and tigers.

3. Have some of the circus animal shapes cut out for the children to color. Then let the children paste these animals onto tongue depressors to make stick puppets.

4. Some parts of the animals may be cut and reattached using paper fasteners to allow for moving parts, such as an elephant's trunk, a giraffe's neck, or a monkey's tail. Discuss how these animals perform in the circus.

Variations/Ways to Extend:

- Read *The Circus* by Brian Wildsmith (New York: Oxford, 1970).
- Let the children make their own depictions of circus animals using crayons, paints, or markers.

II–132 MY CIRCUS PICTURE

Subject Area: Art

Concepts/Skills: Paints with a large brush
Explores a new technique

Objective: The children will use stencils to paint a circus picture.

Materials:
- Circus figures (see patterns)
- Clear self-stick vinyl
- Tempera paints
- Brushes
- Construction paper
- Heavy cardboard
- Scissors
- Tape
- Opaque projector

Procedure:

1. Use the opaque projector to enlarge the circus figures onto cardboard. Use other figures as well for a variety of templates.
2. Cover both sides of the templates with clear self-stick vinyl for easy clean-up and longer wear. Then carefully cut out the figures to form templates.
3. Let the children choose which templates they want to use and help them tape each one in place on their construction paper.
4. Have the children paint inside the template onto the paper. Let the paint partially dry before choosing another template. If the templates are small, tell the children that they may have several circus figures on their paper.

Variations/Ways to Extend:

- Let the children experiment with another type of painting. Tell the children that they may paint any circus scene they want. Encourage them to apply the paint thickly in some areas. Then let them use the handle tip of the brush to scratch lines into the circus painting. Ask them to notice what happens.
- Listen to "Children of All Ages" from the album *Ringling Brothers Barnum & Bailey Circus* (available from Pickwick Records Division, Woodbury, NY 11797).

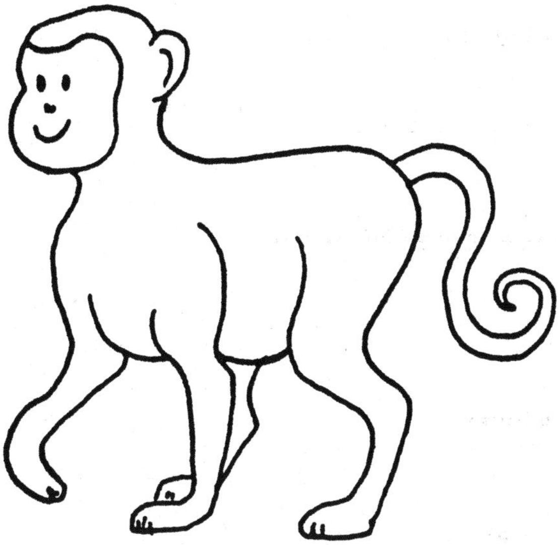

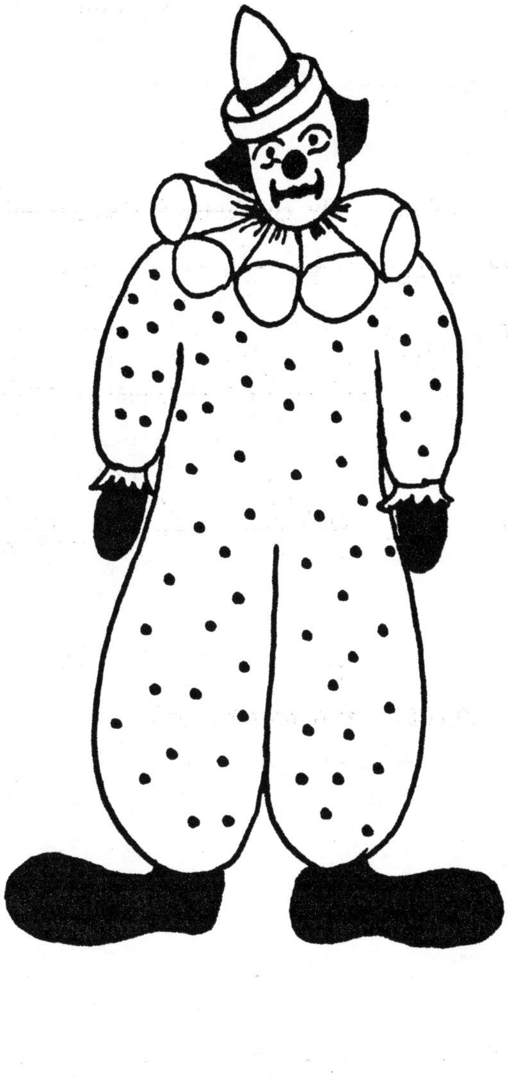

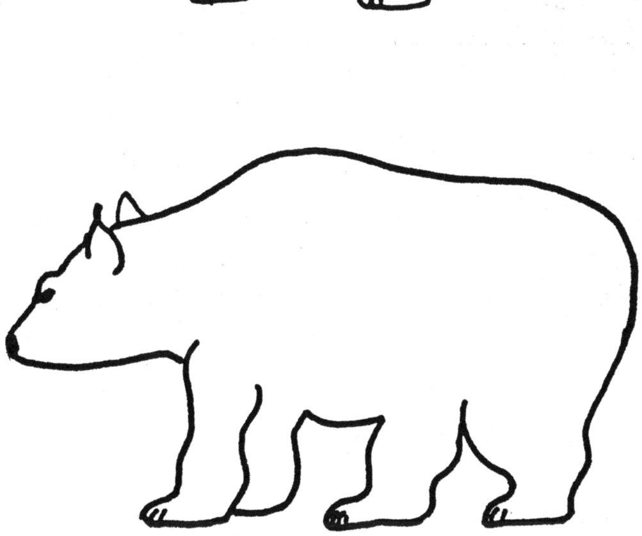

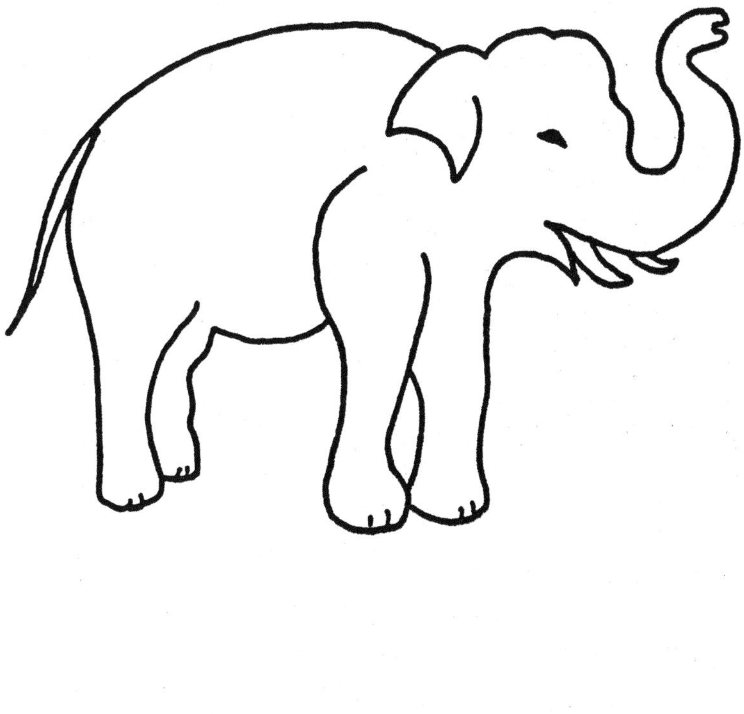

II-133 THIS LITTLE CLOWN

Subject Area: Language Arts

Concept/Skill: Memorizes and repeats a fingerplay

Objective: The children will demonstrate a fingerplay about clowns.

Material: • Words to the fingerplay

Procedure:

1. Teach the following fingerplay to the children:

   This little clown loves to play. (*hold up and wiggle thumb*)
   This little clown does tricks all day. (*hold up and wiggle index finger*)
   This little clown is tall and strong. (*hold up and wiggle middle finger*)
   This little clown sings a funny song. (*hold up and wiggle ring finger*)
   This little clown is wee and small (*hold up and wiggle little finger*)
   But he can do anything at all!

2. Repeat this fingerplay several times with the children.

Variations/Ways to Extend:

- Read *Corduroy* by Don Freeman (New York: Penguin, 1976).
- Make clown hand puppets with the children. You can use clean old socks and decorate them.

II–134   CIRCUS GAMES

Subject Area: Gross Motor Games

Concepts/Skills: Throws a beanbag at a target
Develops body coordination

Objectives: The children will engage in some active beanbag games and pretend to be in the circus.

Materials:
- Beanbags
- Target
- Scissors
- Large clown face
- Markers
- Box

Procedure:

1. Tell the children to pretend that they are in the circus and will do tricks, much as jugglers do. Let the children perform these beanbag activities individually or in small groups.

   - How many ways can you hold a beanbag? (with hand, arm, foot, head) Try them.
   - When the beanbag is on your head, can you walk? Run? Jump?
   - How can you catch a beanbag? (with one hand, two hands, foot)
   - Can you play catch with the beanbag? Try to toss it to one another.
   - Can you toss the beanbag into a container? (Decorate the outside of a box to look like a circus tent.)

2. Make a clown face on a large piece of cardboard or oaktag. Cut out a large opening for the mouth. Tape the face to a heavy open box at ground level and let each child try to throw a beanbag through the mouth. See that everyone has success at doing this.

Variation/Way to Extend:

- Listen to a recording of Aaron Copeland's "Circus Music" from *Red Pony Ballet* to set the atmosphere for this activity.

II–135 CIRCUS TENT

Subject Area: Math

Concept/Skill: Constructs sets of blocks when given a model

Objective: The children will duplicate a block construction to form a circus structure.

Materials:
- Unit blocks
- Accessories

Procedure:

1. Tell the children that they are going to use the block corner today to build a circus tent.
2. Using the unit blocks, work with the children to build a simple structure. Show how to make two rows on the floor and then a row on top of each. Let the children work on the problems of bridging—connecting the two rows with the other blocks placed across to enclose the space and making a roof for the tent.
3. Let the children use some accessories with the tent, such as little wooden animals or a blanket for the "big top."

Variation/Way to Extend:

- Read the poem "Block City" by Robert Louis Stevenson.

BLOCK CITY

What are you able to build with your blocks?
Castles and palaces, temples and docks.
Rain may keep raining, and others go roam,
But I can be happy and building at home.

Let the sofa be mountains, the carpet be sea,
There I'll establish a city for me:
A kirk and a mill and a palace beside,
And a harbor as well where my vessels may ride.

Great is the palace with pillar and wall,
A sort of a tower on the top of it all,
And steps coming down in an orderly way
To where my toy vessels lie safe in the bay.

SPRING

- ○ A New Beginning
- ○ Plant Life
- ○ Air, Rain, and Sunshine
- ○ The Balance of Nature

II–136   SPRING MATCH-UPS

Subject Area: Math

Concepts/Skills: Places objects on their outlines
Predicts which object will match which outlined shape

Objective: The children will match spring objects to their respective outlines on paper.

Materials: • Oaktag
• Broad-tip black marker
• Objects from nature

Procedure:

1. Collect on a walk or have the children bring in objects that emphasize the coming of spring, a season of new life and growth. Such items might include old bird nests, small toy rabbits or chickens, large seeds, and leaves.
2. Trace these objects with a black marker onto oaktag.
3. Ask the children to take turns matching each object to its outline.

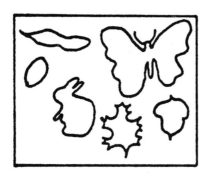 

Variations/Ways to Extend:

• If this activity is difficult for some children, vary it by first tracing basic shapes from blocks onto the oaktag. Use rectangles, squares, circles, and triangles.
• As background music this week, listen to "Spring Song" by Mendelssohn (available from RCA Basic Record, Library for Elementary Schools, 72 Fifth Avenue, New York, NY 10011).

II–137   WHICH EGG?

Subject Area: Thinking Game

Concepts/Skills: Identifies a missing item
Develops color discrimination

Objective: The children will determine which egg has been removed from a basket of colored eggs.

Materials: • Basket
• Plastic eggs in assorted colors

Procedure:

1.   Have the children sit on the floor in a circle. Position the basket of eggs in the center.
2.   Ask one child to cover his or her eyes while another child removes one egg from the basket and puts it out of sight. Ask the first child to guess which egg was removed. **Note: Begin with three eggs, adding one at a time until you are playing with six or more.**

Variations/Ways to Extend:

• Use the eggs to practice position words, such as "The egg is in (behind, next to, under, in front of) the basket."
• Use the eggs for counting experiences.
• Read *The Wonderful Egg* by Dahlov Ipcar (New York: Doubleday, 1958).

II–138 CHICKS

Subject Area: Art

Concepts/Skills: Explores new materials
Develops fine motor movements of pasting and drawing

Objective: The children will create two-dimensional pictures of chicks.

Materials:
- Cotton balls
- Small paper bags
- Yellow powdered tempera paint
- Paste
- Construction paper
- Crayons
- Large jars with lids (optional)

Procedure:

1. Let each child place three cotton balls into a bag containing some yellow powdered tempera paint. Fold the top of the bag over once or twice and let the child shake the bag to coat the cotton balls with yellow powdered tempera. (Note: Try this in large lidded jars so that the children can see the cotton balls turn yellow.)
2. Have the children glue two of the cotton balls together to form a body on the construction paper. Add another cotton ball for the head.
3. With a crayon, have the children draw a beak at the head and two legs and feet under the body. Add some grass or flowers with the crayons.

Variations/Ways to Extend:

- Locate a resource person (a parent or someone from a local hatchery, farm, or pet store) who can bring in some live chicks for the children to see.
- Introduce the children to some poetry related to the monthly theme. Some examples are "Spring Is a New Beginning" by Joan W. Anglund and "The April Rain Song" by Langston Hughes.

II-139 CLOTHES FOR SPRING

Subject Area: Language Arts

Concepts/Skills: Recalls three objects visually presented
Identifies what is missing

Objectives: The children will identify pictures of spring items and participate in a "what is missing" game.

Materials:
- Flannelboard
- Felt
- Clothes catalog pictures
- Fabric glue
- Scissors

Procedure:

1. Cut out pictures from a clothes catalog that show appropriate attire for spring (lightweight dresses, shirts, slacks, sweaters, jackets, rain gear, and so on).
2. Glue the pictures onto felt pieces so that they will adhere to the flannelboard.
3. Discuss with the children the individual pictures and why the clothes are appropriate for us to wear during the spring months.
4. Let the children select three pictures and put them on the flannelboard. Tell the children to cover their eyes while you remove a picture. Ask the children to guess which picture is missing.

Variation/Way to Extend:

- Ask the children to cut out pictures of spring clothing and let them make a collage.

II–140 SPRING RAINBOWS

Subject Area: Music

Concepts/Skills: Listens to and follows directions
Participates in an activity
Recognizes colors

Objectives: The children will listen to a recording, follow the instructions given, and color rainbows.

Materials:
- Song entitled "Color Concoctions" from the album *Color Me a Rainbow* (Melody House) *or* a teacher-made tape
- Crayons
- Paper

Procedure:

1. Distribute the paper and crayons to the children as they gather to listen to the song. Point out the green, blue, red, and yellow crayons. Show the children how to color in arcs to resemble rainbows.
2. Encourage the children to listen carefully to the directions being given on the record and to follow the instructions. (If the song is not available, make your own tape by playing soft background music as you record your own instructions, such as "Make a big circle with the red crayon" or "Use your blue crayon to make a straight line.")
3. Display the completed rainbow pictures at the children's eye-level.

Variation/Way to Extend:

- Use the children's pictures to make a "Welcome Spring" bulletin board display at the children's eye-level. Add some pussywillows or the children's cut-out pictures of flowers, birds, eggs, and bunnies to complete the display.

II–141 BAKING WITH SEEDS

Subject Area: Nutrition and Food Experience

Concepts/Skills: Understands that most plants make seeds for new plants
Develops fine motor movements of kneading, measuring, and pouring
Follows directions

Objectives: The children will prepare and bake muffins and top them with seeds.

Materials:
- Bean seed
- Baking utensils
- Oven
- 1 cup warm water
- 1 package dried yeast
- 1 tablespoon sugar or ½ tablespoon honey
- 1 teaspoon salt
- 2 cups flour
- Poppy seeds
- Sesame seeds

Procedure:

1. Begin a discussion with the children about how life comes from seeds. Open up a bean seed to show the tiny plant inside. Talk about how there are some seeds that we plant to grow food and other seeds that can be eaten just as they are (poppy seeds, sesame seeds, sunflower seeds, pumpkin seeds, and caraway seeds). Discuss each.

2. Now begin to mix the muffins. Let the children measure and mix together the flour, salt, and sugar (or honey). Add the warm water and yeast mixture. Knead the dough on a lightly floured surface. Break into balls and put into greased muffin tins. Sprinkle poppy and sesame seeds on top and let the dough rise. Then bake at 350° F for twenty minutes. (Caution: Be sure the children stay away from the heat.)

3. Let the children enjoy these seeded muffins with milk or juice at snack time.

Variations/Ways to Extend:

- Help the children in understanding how flowers come from seeds by filling with soil one planting pot per two to three children. Make a small hole near the center and put two or three marigold seeds in it. Cover with the soil, place in sunshine, and water daily. Have the children observe the plant's growth.

- Teach the children the following fingerplay:

  I take my little shovel, (*pretend to hold shovel*)
  I dig a hole this way, (*make digging motion*)
  I put the little seeds in deep, (*make sprinkling and patting motions*)
  And then turn on the spray. (*pretend to use spray hose*)

II–142   SWEET POTATO PLANT

Subject Area: Science

Concepts/Skills: Observes, compares, and records
Understands one-to-one correspondence
Understands that plants grow roots, stems, and leaves

Objectives: The children will grow sweet potato plants and record the changes in booklets.

Materials:
- Sweet potatoes, one for each child
- Small jars
- Toothpicks
- Paper
- Paper fasteners
- Water

Procedure:

1. Fill the jars ⅔ full with water and place a sweet potato (narrow end down) into each jar. Secure the potatoes in place with toothpicks.

2. Place the jars in a warm, dark place and add water when necessary. When a stem appears, place the jar in a sunny window and let the children observe the growth occurring each day.

3. Help each child construct a booklet of several pages and make a sweet potato cutout. Let the children paste the cutouts in their books and, as the leaves begin to sprout, likewise paste or color the same number of paper leaves on the sweet potato picture. On subsequent pages, write down the children's words expressing their observations and ideas about their plants.

Variation/Way to Extend:

- Use sweet potatoes in a foods experience. Trim the stem ends and scrub each potato well. Quarter each potato and place in a steamer basket over boiling water in a pot. Steam approximately eight minutes. Serve with pats of butter for a nutritious, delicious snack that's packed with vitamin A. (**Caution:** Be sure the children stay away from the heat.)

II–143 TEXTURED PAINTINGS

Subject Area: Art

Concepts/Skills: Expresses self creatively
Explores and uses new materials

Objective: The children will use colored, textured materials to represent an outdoor scene.

Materials:
- Paper
- Sand or sawdust (from a lumber yard or wood-working shop—be sure it is *not* redwood sawdust)
- Blue, green, and yellow powdered tempera paints
- Glue
- Containers with lids

Procedure:

1. Mix the sand or the sawdust with the powdered paints. Make containers of blue, green, and yellow sand or sawdust.
2. Encourage the children to think about a beautiful spring day with grass and flowers beginning to blossom.
3. Help the children spread glue onto their papers. Then have them sprinkle some blue for sky and green for grass. Help the children mix colors for flowers and trees.
4. When dry, shake off the excess sand or sawdust and display the textured paintings at the children's eye-level.

Variations/Ways to Extend:

- Take a nature walk with the children to observe plant life. Have the children notice all the evidence of spring growth (birds, grass, crocuses, tulips, and so on). Look for seeds, especially the winged seed of the maple tree.
- For an object of real beauty reflecting this month's theme, obtain an 11″ × 14″ reproduction of "The Artist's Garden at Vetheuil" (#2417) by Claude Monet from the National Gallery of Art, Publications Service, Washington, DC 20565. Be sure to write for a catalog and prices.

II–144   IF I WERE A SEED

Subject Area: Creative Movement

Concepts/Skills: Develops sensory-motor abilities
Sequences
Responds to prepositions in directions

Objective: The children will improvise actions to demonstrate their thoughts about a growing seed.

Materials: • Large open area
• Instrumental background music

Procedure:

1. As a warm-up exercise, put on a favorite instrumental recording and encourage the children to be tall and upright trees that are ever so gently swaying in the breeze. Have the children bend from side to side.

2. Instruct the children to think of themselves as tiny seeds. Say that someone has planted them in a nice warm earth, so ask the children to begin by being in a curled-up position. Say that soon it rains on them and then the sun shines, so ask the children to start uncurling and "sprouting" a little.

3. Continue with the rest of the story: "More rain, sunshine, and minerals from the soil allow you to grow steadily, day by day. Soon you are tall, beautiful flowers standing in the sunshine. Suddenly, there is a heavy downfall. It rains so hard that you bend toward the ground. Again, the sun returns and you gradually dry out and stand tall."

Variation/Way to Extend:

• As a science experience, gather some Queen Anne's lace or lily of the valley flowers. Mix one cup of water to every fifteen drops of food coloring. Place the cut stems of the flowers into the colored water and watch the color rise to the flowers. Explain to the children that this shows how a plant takes in nutrients.

II-145 GROCERY STORE

Subject Area: Math

Concepts/Skills: Understands idea of parts and the whole
Rote counts
Compares size and shape
Sorts objects into two categories

Objectives: The children will identify fruits and dramatize a shopping experience that emphasizes math skills.

Materials:
- Store props
- Fresh fruits
- Paper plates
- Paper
- Pencils
- Boxes

Procedure:

1. Set up a grocery store where children can examine, count, purchase, and eat various fruits. Use a cash register, scales, play money, pictures, and other props to let the children engage in dramatic play situations on their own.
2. For other math activities, you might have the children count bunches of grapes and then eat them, or make drawings of small and large, long and short, and round and oval fruits.
3. Let the children experience a coconut by splitting it, draining it, examining the pieces, and eating it.
4. Set up a sorting area in the store. Label two boxes with "Things to Eat" and "Things to Drink." Place cards with pictures of various food items and beverages in the area. Have the children sort by putting the picture cards into the appropriate boxes.

Variations/Ways to Extend:

- Use the coconut shell during music by puncturing it and stringing it. Strike it with a drumstick to use as a percussion instrument.
- Mention to the children that the coconut is an example of a very large seed that grows into a coconut tree.

II–146 PARACHUTE FUN

Subject Area: Gross Motor Games

Concepts/Skills: Walks on tiptoe
Jumps
Hops on one foot
Understands air is everywhere

Objective: The children will conclude that air moves things by observing its effect on a light material.

Materials:
- Nylon parachute or other lightweight fabric
- Large open area
- Foam balls

Procedure:

1. Use a large oval or square piece of the material to play games with the entire group of children. Begin by forming a large circle around the fabric. Ask the children to pick it up by the rim. Let them lift the parachute and lower it, wave it, and wiggle it to see the effects of air on the light material.

2. Throw some foam balls into the center and bounce them on the material. Move in a circle to the right, then to the left, all the while holding tightly to the fabric. Walk in place (fast, slow, quietly, noisily), walk on tiptoe, jump as high as possible, crouch down low, and hop on one foot and then the other while holding onto the parachute.

Variations/Ways to Extend:

- Listen to a recording of Rimsky-Korsakov's "Flight of the Bumblebee" while doing this activity.
- Provide the children with twelve squares of lightweight fabric that have strings attached to each corner. Tie these strings to a wooden spool or beads. Drop these home-made parachutes from up high to see how parachutes work.

- Examine dandelion or milkweed seeds, which are nature's parachutes in action! A book that explains this in simple detail is *Dandelion* by Ladislav Svatos (New York: Doubleday, 1976).

II-147   THE RAINMAKERS

Subject Area: Science

Concept/Skill: Observes a transformation

Objective: The children will observe the process of making rain.

Materials:
- Heat source
- Ice cubes
- Potholders
- Pot of water
- Chilled plate

Procedure:

1. Bring a pot of water to a boil. (**Caution:** Be sure the children stay away from the heat.)
2. Place several ice cubes on the chilled plate and, using potholders, hold the plate above the steam rising from the boiling water. Have the children carefully notice the droplets that form on the bottom of the plate and fall back into the pot.

3. Explain that the steam is warm air rising. When it meets the cool air around the plate, droplets are formed. This is similar to the moisture in a cloud that causes rain.

Variation/Way to Extend:

- Teach the traditional nursery rhyme "Little Drops of Water":
      Little drops of water,
      Little grains of sand,
      Make a mighty ocean
      And the pleasant land.

II–148   SUN CARDS

Subject Area: Math

Concept/Skill: Puts a set of objects in order.

Objective: The children will demonstrate putting a set of color cards in order from lightest to darkest.

Materials:
- Oaktag
- White, yellow, and orange crayons
- Scissors

Procedure:

1. Make a set of five cards, each with a large bright sun pictured in the center. Color the cards with a combination of white, yellow, and orange crayons so that the result is a gradation of color from a pale yellow to a bright golden sun.
2. Have the children take turns placing these in order from lightest to darkest in color.

Variations/Ways to Extend:

- Make another set of sun cards, this time all the same color but gradually varied in size. Let the children place these in order from smallest to largest and then the opposite way.

- Read *Sun Up* by Alvin R. Tresselt (New York: Lothrop, 1949).

Weekly Subtheme: Air, Rain, and Sunshine

II–149 WINDY DAY FUN

Subject Area: Art

Concepts/Skills: Follows directions
Develops fine motor movements of painting and cutting

Objectives: The children will construct and paint box kites to fly outdoors and observe the effects of wind.

Materials:
- Large paper bags, one for each child
- Hole puncher
- Fishline cut in five-foot lengths
- Books
- Scissors
- Streamers
- Paints
- Brushes

Procedure:

1. Help each child fold a two-inch lip around the rim of the bag.
2. Open the bag and place a book inside to make the bag stand up while the child paints and decorates it on all four sides. Add streamers for fun.
3. When the bag is dry, cut off the bottom, leaving the four sides attached.
4. Choose a spot along the folded rim and punch a hole. Tie a length of fishline through here.
5. Take the box kites outdoors on a windy day and let the children run with them.

Variations/Ways to Extend:

- You might want to have the children use fancier kites bought or borrowed. Compare the flying capabilities of the box kites with those of some dragon, delta, and diamond kites.
- Read *Gilberto and the Wind* by Marie H. Ets (New York: Penguin, 1969).

II-150   RAIN

Subject Area: Language Arts

Concepts/Skills: Names plural form of words in poem
Listens to a poem

Objective: The children will recall the words to a verse about rain.

Materials
• Words to the poem
• Oaktag
• Marker
• Pictures

Procedure:

1. Locate the words to the poem "Rain" by Robert Louis Stevenson.

RAIN

The rain is raining all around,
It falls on field and tree,
It rains on the umbrellas here,
And on the ships at sea.

2. Print the poem on a large sheet of oaktag and teach the children this poem by using visual aids.
3. Place pictures of a field, tree, umbrellas, and ships near the corresponding words on each line. Ask the children to repeat the lines with you.

Variations/Ways to Extend:

• Read the Caldecott Honor book *Umbrella* by Taro Yashima (New York: Viking, 1958).
• Distribute maracas to the children and let them accompany the words to the poem with the sound of the maracas.
• For another delightful poem about rain, see "The Umbrella Brigade" by Laura E. Richards, found in her book *Tirra Lirra: Rhymes Old and New* (Boston: Little, Brown, 1955).

II–151 PARTS OF NATURE

Subject Area: Math

Concepts/Skills: Sorts objects into categories
Understands number concepts

Objectives: The children will sort objects by their likenesses and count the number of objects in each group.

Materials:
- Plastic bags, one for each child
- String

Procedure:

1. Take the children on a walk to a wooded area, such as a nearby woods or park. Give them each a small plastic bag and assist them in finding leaves, acorns, twigs, small rocks, and other "pieces" of nature.
2. Upon returning to the classroom, ask the children to sort their objects. Assist any child who may need help.
3. Give the children pieces of string that have been tied together to form circles so that each group (leaves, rocks, etc.) can be separated.

4. Encourage the children to count the number of items in each set.

Variations/Ways to Extend:

- Write an experience chart summarizing what the children found, such as "We found five leaves."
- If possible, visit a nearby stream and observe the surrounding life. Upon returning to the classroom, read *The Clean Brook* by Margaret F. Bartlett (New York: Harper and Row, 1960).

II–152 TOUCH NATURE BAG

Subject Area: Language Arts

Concept/Skill: Demonstrates accurate sense of touch

Objectives: The children will explore various objects from nature through their sense of touch and use this information to identify common objects.

Materials:
- Small pillowcase
- Pairs of objects from nature (two leaves, two similar rocks, two blades of grass, two twigs, two flowers, etc.)

Procedure:

1. Make a nature bag using a small pillowcase and place in it pairs of objects found outdoors. Use items easily found in your area.
2. Ask each child to pick one item out of the bag and then try to find its match in the bag.
3. Encourage the children to talk about the way the object feels, such as its hardness or softness, its texture (smooth, rough, scratchy), its size, its shape, and so on.

Variation/Way to Extend:

- Read *Mr. Gumpy's Outing* by John Burningham (New York: Penguin, 1984). Afterward, ask the children if they ever had an experience similar to that in the book. Or ask the children what they like to explore outdoors.

II-153 LOOK AND REMEMBER

Subject Area: Nutrition

Concepts/Skills: Points to appropriate color upon command
Identifies what is missing
Matches shapes

Objective: The children will understand that fruits are part of nature.

Materials:
- Apples, oranges, and bananas
- Serving tray
- Knife
- Paper plates

Procedure:

1. Briefly discuss the fact that fruits come from nature. Explain that apples, oranges, and bananas all grow on trees. Also explain that fruits are an important part of our diets because they give us vitamins and energy and help us grow. Ask, "Which fruit do you like best?"

2. Ask the children to identify the colors of the fruits you show them. Then compare the fruits' shapes. Ask, "Which fruit is the most different in shape?" Conclude that the apple and orange are almost round.

3. Play the "Look and Remember" game. Place the three fruits on a tray. Have the children look at the fruits very carefully and then ask them to close their eyes. Remove one fruit and ask the children to guess which one is missing. Once the children are able to do this with three fruits, try four and then five fruits.

4. End the activity by slicing the fruits for a nutritious snack.

Variation/Way to Extend:

- Use red and yellow tempera paints in an art activity with the children. Give them some pre-cut apple shapes to paint red and some pre-cut banana shapes to paint yellow. Demonstrate how the red and yellow paints can be mixed to obtain orange and then give the children pre-cut orange shapes to paint. Let the children experiment with colors by mixing eyedroppers of food coloring into big jars of water.

II–154   BIRD CLASSIFICATION

Subject Area: Thinking Games

Concept/Skill: Sorts objects into two different categories

Objective: The children will classify pictures of birds into two categories.

Material: • Pictures of birds

Procedure:.

1.   Gather eight to ten pictures of various kinds of birds. Be sure that the pictured birds differ in size and color.
2.   In a group, show the children each picture and have them identify it as a bird. Ask them if the bird is big or little and have the children sort the birds on the basis of size.
3.   Then have the children sort the pictured birds on the basis of color. You might, for example, say, "Put all the birds with some red here and all others there."

Variations/Ways to Extend:

• Using pieces of string, allow the children to make necklaces using doughnut-shaped cereal. Tell the children that they can wear the necklaces and then, after lunch or snack, take them outside and hang them from branches for birds to eat. Talk about the importance of providing food for and taking care of birds.

• Read the Caldecott Medal book *Song of the Swallows* by Leo Politi (New York: Scribner's, 1949).

II–155   WHAT DO ANTS EAT?

Subject Area: Science

Concepts/Skills: Observes objects closely
Understands sentences and questions as indicated by relevant responses

Objective: The children will observe that ants rely on eating foods from their surroundings.

Materials:
- Shovel
- Wide-mouth quart jar
- Dark paper
- Tape
- Old nylon stocking
- Cotton balls
- Scissors
- Water
- Rubber band

Procedure:

1. With the children, find an anthill outside. Using a small shovel, carefully dig some of the dirt out and place it at the bottom of the jar.
2. Have the children wet several cotton balls and place these inside the jar. Keep the cotton balls wet by dropping water through the nylon stocking every day.
3. Back inside the classroom, cover the outside of the jar with a sheet of dark paper fastened with tape and use a piece of old nylon stocking and a rubber band to cover the top of the jar.

4. Take the children on another walk outside and ask them to find food for the ants, such as blades of grass and leaves. You might also include bread crumbs, jam, and corn meal. (Ants will eat practically anything!)
5. After three days, remove the black paper to observe the ants. Encourage the children to describe their observations. Check the bottom of the jar as well.
6. After the observations, replace the paper around the jar. Ask, "What foods did the ants eat?" (Make the point that ants will eat foods that surround them.) "What have the ants done?" (Note tunnels and how the ants move about for gathering food and carrying eggs.)
7. After a week of observation, help the children carefully replace the ants back outdoors.

Variation/Way to Extend:

- Read *The Way of an Ant* by Kazue Mizumura (New York: Harper and Row, 1970).

COMMUNITY WORKERS

○ Health Professionals—

    Doctors, Nurses, Dentists

○ Police Officers and Firefighters

○ Shopkeepers and Office Workers

○ Librarians and Postal Workers

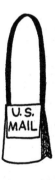

II–156   WHAT DOCTORS DO

Subject Area: Gross Motor Games

Concept/Skill: Understands prepositions

Objectives: The children will play a game and use prepositions while learning about what doctors do.

Materials: • Book
• Cot
• Pillow
• Stethoscope
• Pen light

Procedure:

1. Read *My Friend the Doctor* by Jane Werner Watson et al. (New York: Western, 1972) and discuss the story with the children.
2. Gather the children around a cot with a pillow. Tell the children that they are going to pretend they are in a doctor's office.
3. Ask each child to take a turn performing one of the following behaviors. Be sure to emphasize the positional words.

   Sit "on" the cot.
   Get "under" the blanket.
   Get "off" of the cot.
   Go "over" the cot.
   Stand "in front of" the cot (away from pillow).
   Stand "in back of" the cot (near pillow).
   Touch the "top" of the cot.
   Touch the "bottom" of the cot.
4. Now take a stethoscope and pen light and ask each child to:

   Take the pen light and look "in" someone else's ear.
   Place the stethoscope "on" someone else's heart and listen.

Variation/Way to Extend:

• Glue pictures of male and female doctors onto cardboard and cut each picture into several pieces. Ask the children to put these puzzles together. Code the backs of all the pieces of one puzzle with the same number for easy identification and keep the pieces in envelopes.

II–157 SAY "AH"

Subject Area: Creative Dramatics

Concepts/Skills: Describes action taking place in pictures
Tells use of pictured items
Points to and names body parts
Plays using symbols

Objectives: The children will listen to a story about the hospital and engage in related role play using props.

Materials:
- Book
- Dolls
- Tongue depressors
- White, adult-sized shirts
- Egg cartons
- Play telephone
- Eyeglass frames
- String
- Surgical stocking caps
- Tape
- Pads and pencils
- Toy doctor's bag
- Baby scale
- Plastic bottles
- Tape measure
- Bandages
- Play syringes
- Markers

Procedure:

1. Draw lines on some tongue depressors and pretend that they are thermometers.
2. String a single section of an egg carton onto a long length of string and pretend that it is a stethoscope.
3. Read *Jeff's Hospital Book* by Harriet L. Sobol (New York: Walck, 1975), which shows real photographs of a boy in a hospital. Encourage the children to describe the action seen in the pictures of this book. Mention the equipment pictured and talk about their uses. Allow the children to share their experiences (if any) of being in the hospital if they so desire.
4. Set up all the materials listed and have the children play doctor, nurse, admissions clerk, nurse's aide, and other figures from the story.
5. Ask the children to point to or name parts of the body (head, hands, arms, legs, knees, feet, and facial features) as they examine one another or dolls. Tell the children that as doctors they should explain to their patients what are the functions of the major body parts, such as what we can do with our hands, how we breathe through the nose, how our heart pumps blood, and so on.

Variation/Way to Extend:

- Read *My Doctor* by Harlow Rockwell (New York: Macmillan, 1973).

Weekly Subtheme: Health Professionals (Doctors, Nurses, Dentists)

II–158   LET'S TALK ABOUT TEETH

Subject Area: Language Arts

Concepts/Skills: Tells own name, sex, and age
Understands sentences and questions
Recalls

Objectives: The children will hear about and discuss good dental care by visiting a dentist.

Materials: • Book
• Dentist

Procedure:

1. Read *Our Tooth Story: A Tale of Twenty Teeth* by Ethel Kessler and Leonard Kessler (New York: Dodd, 1972), which explains the instruments and equipment used by both male and female dentists.
2. Discuss with the children the foods and practices that are necessary for maintaining strong, healthy teeth.
3. Make arrangements with a local dentist for a visit by the children. Try to have each child introduce him- or herself to the dentist, giving his or her name, sex, and age.
4. Help the children identify items they see in the dentist's office, based on their having seen them in the book.

Variation/Way to Extend:

• Upon returning to the classroom from the dentist's office, let the children pretend to be dentists. Supply the necessary props.

Weekly Subtheme: Health Professionals (Doctors, Nurses, Dentists)

II–159 TOOTHY MOUTH

Subject Area: Art

Concepts/Skills: Explores media
Develops fine motor movement of printing

Objective: The children will print with potato cut-outs.

Materials:
- Felt-tip pens
- Potatoes
- Knife
- Black construction paper
- White paint

Procedure:

1. Ask the children to use felt-tip pens to draw large open mouths with no teeth on the black paper.
2. Cut the potatoes in half, and into each half cut away the potato to resemble teeth. Distribute these halves to the children.
3. Let the children dip the potatoes into the white paint and help them print the teeth inside their drawn mouths.
4. Talk about the dentist's job of helping people care for their teeth.

Variations/Ways to Extend:

- Make a paper frame for the children's "toothy mouths." Take a square piece of paper that is larger than the drawing and fold it diagonally in both directions to clearly see the midpoint of the paper. Bring each of the four corners to the center point and fold. Then open up the folded corners to make a frame. Help the children cut their drawings to fit the rectangle inside the frame and paste in place.
- Read the Caldecott Honor book *One Morning in Maine* by Robert McCloskey (New York: Viking, 1952).
- Make a collaborative book about the children and their teeth. Write down stories they may have about "new teeth" or "hurt teeth" or siblings' "lost teeth."

II–160   CLAY TEETH

Subject Area: Social Studies

Concept/Skill: Develops fine motor movements of rolling and pinching

Objectives: The children will help to prepare a recipe for clay and create teeth for a face.

Materials:
- Pre-cut oaktag faces (see pattern)
- 2 cups flour
- 1 cup water
- 1 cup salt
- 1 tablespoon oil
- Glue
- Crayons or paints
- Pencils (optional)

Procedure:

1. Mix the flour, water, salt, and oil well and knead to a dough-like consistency.
2. Have the children make little balls and then press indentations with fingers or pencils to form teeth.
3. Leave these out overnight so that the clay will dry hard.
4. Let the children glue the dried teeth onto a face that they can then color or paint.

Variations/Ways to Extend:

- Read *My Dentist* by Harlow Rockwell (New York: Greenwillow, 1975).
- Let the children use hand mirrors to see how their teeth line up and how they have different shapes.
- Mention to the children about the different kinds of teeth we have and the different jobs they do (the front teeth are for cutting, the eyeteeth are for ripping and tearing, and the molars are for smashing and grinding food).

II–161 TRAFFIC KNOW-HOW

Subject Area: Gross Motor Games

Concepts/Skills: Rides a tricycle or other wheel toy
Plays using symbols
Dramatizes

Objective: The children will pretend to be riding on streets and under the direction of police officers.

Materials:
- Tricycles or other wheel toys
- Chalk
- Police officer hats
- Paper tickets
- Small traffic signs (either teacher-made or commercially prepared)

Procedure:

1. Discuss the idea of safety on the roads and why traffic tickets are given.
2. On the playground, draw chalk lines to designate streets and set up small traffic signs.
3. Select one or two children to role play being police officers who direct traffic and issue traffic tickets. Let the other children ride their tricycles or other wheel toys between the chalk lines or "streets" and respond to the officers.

Variation/Way to Extend:

- Walk to an intersection to let the children watch a real police officer or crossing guard direct traffic and observe how it is done.

II-162 POLICE OFFICER VISIT

Subject Area: Social Studies

Concepts/Skills: Understands sentences and questions as indicated by relevant responses
Recognizes and names police officer's clothing and badge

Objective: The children will generalize about the role of the police officer in the community.

Material: • Fully uniformed police officer

Procedure:

1. Invite a police officer to the classroom for a friendly discussion. The officer might show the children his or her motorcycle or car parked outside.
2. Let the children study the officer's hat, uniform, and badge.
3. Ask the officer to talk about safety rules, wearing seat belts, and similar topics. You might also ask the officer to describe a typical day on the job and/or to bring in a piece of equipment used frequently on the job to share with the children.

Variations/Ways to Extend:

• Make traffic lights by painting the inside of bottle caps red, yellow, and green. Glue these onto a cardboard tube.
• Read *What Do You Want to Be?* by Françoise (New York: Scribner's, 1957).

II–163 FIREFIGHTER HATS

Subject Area: Art

Concepts/Skills: Develops fine motor movement of cutting
Role plays

Objective: The children will construct firefighter hats to use to role play.

Materials:
- 12″ × 18″ sheets of red construction paper
- Scissors
- Pencil
- Gold pen
- Lengths of hose or cardboard dowels

Procedure:

1. Draw a large egg shape on a sheet of red paper for each child.
2. Let the children, with your assistance, cut on the line drawn. Cut a semi-circle in the center of each hat for the child's head.

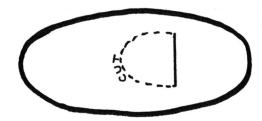

3. Fold a flap up from this to fit on the child's head.
4. Write the child's name or a number in gold ink on the flap.
5. Give the children lengths of hose or cardboard dowels and let them fight pretend fires while wearing their hats.

Variations/Ways to Extend:

- Use white construction paper to make the hats and let the children paint them red.
- Read *Firegirl* by Gibson Rich (Old Westbury, NY: Feminist Press, 1972).

II-164 THE FIREFIGHTER HAD ONE LADDER

Subject Areas: Music and Math

Concepts/Skills: Rote counts
Participates in music

Objective: The children will sing a song about a firefighter.

Materials: • Pictures
• Words to the song

Procedure:

1. Adapt the words to the song according to the pictures of firefighters you have on hand or to equipment with which the children are familiar.

2. Sing the following song to the tune of "Johnny Works with One Hammer." Vary the personal pronoun to project a nonsexist image.

> The firefighter had one ladder, one ladder, one ladder.
> The firefighter had one ladder, and then she had two.
> The firefighter squirted one hose, one hose, one hose,
> The firefighter squirted one hose, and then he squirted two.
> The firefighter swung one ax, one ax, one ax,
> The firefighter swung one ax, and then she swung two.

Variations/Ways to Extend:

• Add toy fire engines and wooden firefighter figures to the block corner. Suggest that the children build a fire station.

• Provide small, sturdy boxes for the children to use as fire engines and round-topped clothespins to use as firefighters.

II-165 THE CANDLE FLAME

Subject Area: Science

Concepts/Skills: Observes objects closely
Describes, compares, and records

Objectives: The children will observe and describe what happens in a candle experiment.

Materials:
- 3 small candles
- 2 glass jars of different sizes
- Metal base
- Matches

Procedure:

1. To show the children that fire has to have air to burn, set up three small candles on a metal base. Do this by melting enough of each candle's bottom to hold it up. (**Caution:** Be sure this experiment is done only by an adult. Keep the children away from the heat.)

2. Light the three candles at the same time and cover two with glass jars of different sizes and let the third burn uncovered.

3. Have the children notice that the two covered candles will soon go out because the air (oxygen) is used up, but the other candle will still be burning. Ask the children to describe what happened. Stimulate their thinking processes by asking such questions as "What did you see?" and "Why do you think that happened?"

Variation/Way to Extend:

- Let the children record their observations by making a tape recording on which they describe what took place.

II–166 GROCERY STORE

Subject Area: Math

Concepts/Skills: Rote counts
Plays using symbols
Sorts objects into two given categories

Objective: The children will engage in math activities while playing "store."

Materials:
- Price signs and labels
- Scales
- Play food
- Cash register
- Play money
- Scissors
- Empty coffee cans
- Small items for counters
- Pre-cut shapes for sorting
- Empty food packages with labels
- Clear self-stick vinyl
- Boxes

Procedure:

1. Discuss going to the grocery store or supermarket with the children. Ask, "What do you see there?" Let them suggest a long list.
2. Tell the children that they are going to play "grocery store."
3. Emphasize prices, scales for weighing, and sizes and shapes of objects. Count out a dozen "eggs" for the children to show how there are twelve. Use the cash register to pretend to pay for goods and to make change. In a sturdy box, set containers (margarine tubs) and fill with various grocery items to use as counters, such as bottle caps, cut-up sponges, macaroni, straws, plastic spoons, corks, and crackers. Use these for a concrete counting experience. Cut up a calendar and let the children use the numbers to represent play money or price signs. Use the scale to weigh different items and let the children sort according to which weigh the same, are heavier, or are lighter. Cover empty coffee cans with clear self-stick vinyl and use these for such specific sorting activities as: large macaroni shells, large lima beans, large boxes of toothpaste, large yellow sponges, small macaroni shells, small lima beans, small boxes of toothpaste, and small yellow sponges.
4. Sorting by size is more difficult than sorting by shape or color because it requires comparison. Let the children practice sorting by size and color by pre-cutting large and small red and green circles from construction paper and asking the children to sort by: large red circles, large green circles, small red circles, and small green circles.

Variation/Way to Extend:

- After the children have finished playing "store," let them engage in a creative art experience by gluing the cardboard food boxes together in free-form structures.

Weekly Subtheme: Shopkeepers and Office Workers

II–167   SHAKY SONG

Subject Area: Music

Concepts/Skills: Solves problems
Listens to different sounds

Objectives: The children will construct instruments from materials found in various stores and offices and use them to accompany a song.

Materials:
- Words and music to song
- Tape
- Tempera paints
- Brushes
- Stapler
- Crayons
- Bells
- Dried lima beans
- Paper cups
- Oatmeal containers
- Yarn
- Scissors
- Glue
- Small blocks of wood
- Medium sandpaper
- Sturdy paper plates
- Shoe boxes
- Rubber bands
- Dowels
- Wooden ice cream sticks
- Rubber sheeting
- Bottle caps

Procedure:

1.   Collect all the materials and ask the children to tell how they think each item is used. Explain to the children that they are going to use the items "in brand new ways" to make musical instruments.

2.   Teach the children "Shaky Song" and let them use the following home-made instruments to accompany the chorus:

Sandpaper blocks—Staple squares of sandpaper onto smooth blocks of wood and rub together.

Paper plate tambourine—Decorate the backs of two sturdy paper plates. Staple them together along three-fourths of the rim. Drop in some small bells or dried lima beans before completely stapling all around. Shake the tambourine to produce a sound.

Banjo or guitar—Stretch rubber bands around an uncovered shoe box. Cut a small hole in one end, push a long dowel through, tape it into place, and then pluck the rubber bands.

Maracas—Place dried lima beans inside a small paper cup and glue another cup on top. Push a wooden ice cream stick through the bottom, tape it into place, and then shake.

Drum—Remove the lid from a round oatmeal container. Punch two holes at opposite sides about two inches down from the rim. String a length of yarn to serve as the drum's neck strap. Cover the hole with a square of rubber sheeting and secure with a rubber band. Pat the top to produce a sound.

Chimes—Paint a collection of bottle caps. (Add glue to the tempera paint to make it adhere to the metal.) Punch holes through the centers of the caps and put lengths of yarn through the holes. Punch holes all around very sturdy paper plates and attach the yarn. Staple a cardboard handle to the top center of the plates to hold. (Try this with canning lid inserts for a different chime-like sound.)

Variation/Way to Extend:

- Use the home-made instruments to practice the musical concept of loud versus soft. Let the children make a sound with the instruments they are holding, first individually and then as a group. Let each child have a turn with each instrument.

Shaky Song

Words and Music by BOB MESSANO
Arranged by John Sheehan

2. Now you shake it twice! *(etc.)*

3. Now you shake it three times! *(etc.)*

4. Now you shake it four times! *(etc.)*

5. Now you shake like a snake! *(etc.)*

II–168 NO-BAKE COOKIES

Subject Area: Nutrition and Foods Experience

Concepts/Skills: Develops fine motor movements of measuring, pouring, mixing, and shaping
Develops sense of touch, smell, and taste

Objectives: The children will help prepare real cookies and pretend to be bakers.

Materials:
- Aprons
- Cooking utensils
- Bowls
- Wax paper
- Spoon
- Heat source
- ½ cup milk
- ¼ pound butter
- 5 tablespoons cocoa
- 2½ cups quick oats
- 1 tablespoon vanilla
- 2 cups sugar (or honey equivalent)

Procedure:

1. Let the children mix the sugar, milk, butter, and cocoa.
2. Bring this to a boil and cook for two minutes. (**Caution:** Be sure the children stay away from the heat.)
3. Remove the pot from the heat source and let the children carefully add the quick oats and vanilla.
4. Beat until stiff and drop onto wax paper by the spoonful. Let cool.
5. Tell the children that the cookies are now ready to eat. Let the children play "bakery" and "sell" cookies to one another before they all enjoy some cookies with milk at snack time.

Variation/Way to Extend:

- Read the poem "The Baker" by J. B. McKinney to the children. Make a wall chart of the poem to be illustrated by the children with cut-out magazine pictures of bakers, pies, loaves of bread, cookies, and similar related items.

II–169 SAWDUST SCULPTURE

Subject Areas: Art and Language Arts

Concepts/Skills: Repeats simple fingerplay
Explores new materials

Objectives: The children will participate in a fingerplay about a carpenter and sculpt from a sawdust mixture.

Materials:
- Words to fingerplay
- Sawdust (do *not* use redwood sawdust)
- Plaster of Paris
- Wallpaper paste
- Water
- Sturdy shirt box
- Squares of heavy cardboard or wood

Procedure:

1. Teach the children the following fingerplay as a stimulus for working with sawdust. (You might want to vary the pronoun each time the fingerplay is repeated so that the children realize that there are also women carpenters.)

   The carpenter's hammer goes tap, tap, tap. (*make hammer motion with hand*)
   His saw goes see, saw, see. (*make back-and-forth sawing motion*)
   He sands and he measures (*smooth with a flat hand*)
   And he saws and he hammers (*repeat motion of tools*)
   While he makes a house for me. (*form peak overhead with arms*)

2. Discuss the job of the carpenter and how sawdust is often a byproduct of his or her work.

3. Have the children sift through the sawdust (easily secured at any lumber yard) to observe its qualities.

4. Let the children help in the preparation of the following sculpture medium and then sculpt onto a piece of heavy cardboard or wood:

   2 cups sawdust
   1 cup plaster of Paris
   ½ cup wallpaper paste
   2 cups water

   Let the children mix the ingredients thoroughly in a sturdy shirt box and then each sculpt. Note: Allow leftover plaster to harden and then discard it. Do *not* pour the mixture into plumbing because serious blockage could occur!

Variations/Ways to Extend:
- Allow the children time in the woodworking area or at least a chance to hammer some nails into fiberboard. (**Caution:** Be sure this is done under adult supervision.)
- Have the children use tempera paints to decorate sanded wood scraps that have been glued together into constructions.
- Provide the children with a cigar box filled with gadgets with which to play, especially lots of large nuts and bolts.

II–170   TO THE MARKET

Subject Area: Social Studies

Concepts/Skills: Names common objects
Determines sequence
Plays using symbols

Objective: The children will dramatize the role of the grocery clerk.

Materials:
- Pictures
- Apron
- Vendor's hat
- Baskets
- Carts
- Play money
- Cash register
- Food boxes
- Wallets and purses
- Pencils and pads
- Plastic fruit and vegetables
- Table or shelves
- Sundries
- Telephone

Procedure:

1. Encourage the children to share in bringing from home empty cartons, cans, egg cartons, and plastic bottles to represent a variety of merchandise found in a grocery store.
2. Form shelves and counters with blocks or cardboard boxes. Display large pictures of grocery stores around the room.
3. Let the children change roles as consumers and suppliers during this dramatic play. Use appropriate props to let the children take a trip to the grocery store to buy food for dinner. Let someone be the cashier and collect the money from the shoppers.
4. Be sure that a good deal of practical language is used in this dramatic play; it might lead the children into trying new types of food.

Variations/Ways to Extend:

- Read *The Supermarket* by Harlow and Anne Rockwell (New York: Macmillan, 1979).
- Look at the pictures in *I Want to Be a Storekeeper* by Carla Greene (Chicago: Childrens, 1958).

II-171 TRIP TO THE LIBRARY

Subject Area: Social Studies

Concepts/Skills: Shows need to investigate and explore
Participates in a group

Objectives: The children will visit their local library and observe the functions it performs as well as the roles of the librarians.

Material: • Trip arrangements

Procedure:

1. In advance of your trip, try to arrange for the children's department of the library to exhibit some of the children's artwork. This is done in many areas where various preschools alternate in using the display area, creating exciting exhibits for the community. Then during the field trip, the children can proudly view their pictures on the wall.

2. Also request a special story time and/or a tour of the library. Let the children observe the arrangement of books. In passing, point out other services that are offered—filmstrip projectors, films, tape and record collections, and sometimes toy collections as well.

3. Try to develop the children's interest in visiting the library and their appreciation of how enjoyable a place it can be.

Variations/Ways to Extend:

• If you cannot arrange this field trip, invite a librarian to visit your class and talk about the library. He or she can bring equipment for an audio-visual presentation or read or tell a story to the children.

• Let the children play "library" in the room's book area.

II-172 OUR CLASS BOOK

Subject Area: Language Arts

Concepts/Skills: Speaks in four- to-six-word sentences
Names concrete objects in the environment

Objectives: The children will construct a book as a group project and develop the idea of a book as a collection of written thoughts.

Materials:
- Construction paper
- Oaktag
- Hole puncher
- Several books
- Yarn or notebook rings
- Pictures
- Marker

Procedure:

1. Although the children should be familiar with books, take some time to let them examine the physical attributes of a book. Point out the front and back covers, the title page, the author's name, and the body of the story in words and pictures. Have them notice that some books' pages are numbered.
2. Begin making a class book with oaktag covers and construction paper pages. Punch holes in the papers and use notebook rings or yarn to fasten the pages together.
3. Ask each child to respond to a stimulus, such as a picture or a field trip, and describe it in his or her own words. Write these responses on the papers. Be sure a different child's entry (labeled with his or her name) appears on each page of the book.
4. Let the children give their book a name (title) and complete a group collage of colorful shapes on the front cover.
5. Display the book in the reading area and read from it frequently.

Variation/Way to Extend:

- Make other class books that concentrate on a particular theme, such as "Our Favorite Toys," to which the children would enjoy contributing.

II–173   POST OFFICE

Subject Area: Creative Dramatics and Movement

Concepts/Skills: Understands the idea of a post office
Develops fine motor movement of cutting
Cooperates in a group
Plays using symbols

Objectives: The children will assist in making mailbags and use them to play "post office."

Materials:
- 18″ × 24″ piece of canvas
- Pinking shears
- Fabric glue
- Ruler
- Pencil
- Props

Procedure:

1. Fold the canvas in half so that you have a 9″ × 12″ piece.
2. With a ruler and pencil, draw a rectangle onto the fabric using the open nine-inch side as a starting point.
3. Let the children help cut around the open sides with the pinking shears. Then glue halfway up both twelve-inch sides so that a child can place the bag on his or her back and put the arms through the straps.
4. Set up a post office in the classroom. Place props (a cash register, play money, scales, rubber stamps, ink pads, used stamps, paper) on a table.
5. Use beverage cartons for sorting letters by color or size. Use junk mail or colored index cards for letters to place in the mailbag and deliver by wagon. Paint or cover cartons to use as mailboxes around the room.

Variation/Way to Extend:

- Provide math experiences by discussing with the children how much a letter weighs, how much a stamp costs, and the ideas of more or less, larger or smaller, heavier or lighter.

II–174   POST OFFICE SHAPES

Subject Area: Math

Concepts/Skills: Recognizes patterns
Matches shapes

Objectives: The children will identify shapes, match them, and complete patterns.

Materials: • Mailbag
• Two envelopes
• Flannelboard
• Several of each pre-cut felt shapes (see patterns)

Procedure:

1.   Gather the children around a flannelboard and discuss some of the post office items familiar to them. As you mention these items, remove one set of pre-cut felt shapes from an envelope in the mailbag and let the children put these on the flannelboard.

2.   Give the second envelope, which also contains a set of the shapes, to a child and have the child select the shape to match yours. For example, if a hat is displayed, the child also displays a hat.

3.   Give each child a chance. Then try patterns. If, for example, you put a hat, then a mailbox, then a hat, then a mailbox, ask, "What comes next?" Let each child have a turn trying different patterns.

Variation/Way to Extend:

• Vary this activity by using such basic shapes as a circle, square, triangle, and rectangle to practice patterning.

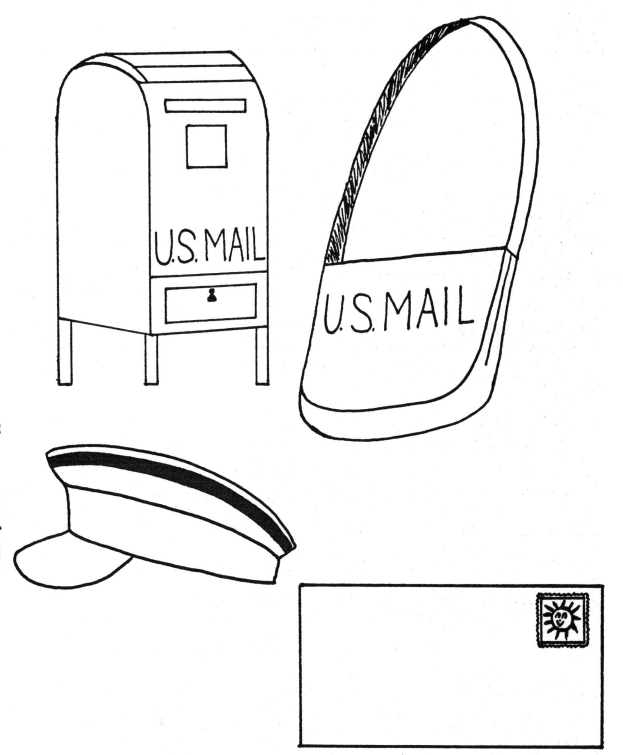

Weekly Subtheme: Librarians and Postal Workers

II–175 MAIL TRUCKS

Subject Area: Art

Concepts/Skills: Explores a new medium
Fingerpaints
Develops a sense of touch

Objectives: The children will fingerpaint on paper cut in the shape of a mail truck.

Materials:
- Liquid laundry starch
- Powdered tempera paints
- Glossy paper
- Containers
- Background music
- Scissors

Procedure:

1. Add liquid laundry starch to powdered tempera paint until a consistency of heavy cream is formed
2. Put the paint in several containers and place them on the art tables.
3. Give each child a piece of glossy paper cut in the shape of a mail truck. Let the children fingerpaint in a leisurely fashion, perhaps to soothing music.
4. When the paintings are dry, display them in the classroom or send them home.

Variation/Way to Extend:

- Collect old stamps that have been steamed, soaked, or cut from envelopes. Also look for holiday stamps and stamps from various organizations. Have the children make a stamp collage from this collection.

SUMMER

- ○ The Ocean, Rivers, and Lakes
- ○ Insects
- ○ Day and Night
- ○ Vacation and Travel

II–176   WHAT'S IN THE OCEAN?

Subject Area: Language Arts

Concepts/Skills: Asks and answers questions
Recalls objects visually presented
Recognizes which does not belong

Objectives: The children will respond to questions about the ocean and play a visual memory game.

Materials:
- Fish-shaped crackers
- Ocean objects and pictures
- Unrelated objects and pictures

Procedure:

1. Begin by distributing a snack of fish-shaped crackers. Discuss where fish can be found (oceans, rivers, lakes). Say, "Today we are going to talk about the ocean. Has anyone been to a beach to see an ocean? What was it like? Did you find anything there? What did you like about it?"

2. Show pictures of ocean waves, surfers, and people swimming in the ocean. Choose one provocative picture and ask, "What questions do you have about this picture?"

3. Place three objects (crab shell, stones, dried starfish) or pictures related to the ocean on the floor. Ask the children to identify each object.

4. Now ask the children to close their eyes while you take an object or picture away. Have the children try to guess which was taken.

5. Then place an object or picture that is unrelated to the ocean and ask the children to guess which does not belong.

Variations/Ways to Extend:

- Ask the children to match similar shells, glue them to a matboard, and paint them with tempera paint.
- Let the children play with the ocean objects in a water table.
- Fill a pretty jar with shells, rocks, beach glass, and water. Place the jar in a sunny window for all to admire.
- Obtain an 11″ × 14″ art reproduction of "The Much Resounding Sea" (#2330) by Thomas Moran from the National Gallery of Art, Publications Service, Washington, DC 20565. Be sure to write for a catalog and prices.

II-177 OCEAN SCAVENGER HUNT

Subject Area: Thinking Games

Concepts/Skills: Names concrete objects
Sorts objects by size
Understands concepts of "big" and "little"

Objectives: The children will identify ocean representations and classify them by size.

Materials:
- Ocean pictures, objects, and models
- Paper
- Marker

Procedure:

1. Collect representations (some real, some models, and some pictures) of ocean life. These can include shells, driftwood, seaweed, pebbles, sand, and sea animals (such as crabs, lobsters, dolphins, whales, starfish, and jellyfish)

2. Show the children these objects and pictures. Help them to identify each object and, by showing pictures of the ocean, explain where they are found.

3. Hide each of the pictures and objects around the classroom. Tell the children they are going on an ocean scavenger hunt, looking for all the objects they have been talking about.

4. If you have a large collection of shells, let the children sort them into two categories for "big" and "little."

Variations/Ways to Extend:

- Prepare a table exhibit of "Ocean Life." Place shells, objects, and pictures on the table, along with magnifying glasses and books, such as *Animals of the Seashore* by Julie Becker (St. Paul, MN: EMC, 1977). Encourage sand play as well.
- Read the Caldecott Honor book *Swimmy* by Leo Lionni (New York: Pantheon, 1963).

II–178   RIVER MOVEMENTS

Subject Area: Gross Motor Games

Concept/Skill: Develops gross motor movements of walking, hopping, and walking on tiptoe

Objectives: The children will be able to identify rivers from pictures and demonstrate gross motor movements.

Materials:
- River pictures
- Masking tape
- Kraft paper
- Blue paint
- Brushes
- Scissors
- Sand table
- Water

Procedure:

1. Cut a long swirl from a roll of kraft paper.
2. Help the children paint the swirl blue to simulate a river and tape it to the floor.
3. Show pictures of rivers and talk a little about each.
4. Have the children gather around the sand table. Slowly pour water on top of the pile of sand, saying, "This could be snow melting on a warm day in the mountains. What is happening?" Continue pouring water. Let the children point out where they see some big rivers, small rivers, and lakes forming.
5. Ask the children to act out the following movements on the paper river. Let the children do the first four movements individually and then the next four in small groups.

   > walk forward
   > jump three times with both feet together
   > hop on one foot
   > walk on tiptoe
   > pretend to be a boat floating down the river
   > pretend to be a frog in the river and jump along
   > pretend to be a worm crawling alongside the river
   > pretend to be a bird flying high above the river

Variation/Way to Extend:

- If possible, take a field trip to a nearby river or stream. Have the children notice how the water flows downstream. Look for any waterfalls or ripples. Ask the children if they can see any fish in the water.

II–179   DRINKING WATER OR SALT WATER?

Subject Area: Science

Concepts/Skills: Understands concepts of "full" and "empty"
Develops sense of taste

Objectives: The children will identify "empty" and "full" and taste the difference between drinking water and salt water.

Materials:
- Paper cups
- Plastic pitchers of drinking water and salt water
- Small shovels
- Sandbox

Procedure:

1. Give each child a paper cup and a small shovel and take them outside to the sandbox. Bring along two plastic pitchers of water, one filled with tap water and the other with water and salt.
2. Sit the children around the sandbox and spend a few minutes talking about oceans. Explain that ocean water is salty.
3. Ask the children if their cups have any water in them. Encourage use of the word "empty."
4. Now fill their cups with drinking water and ask, "Is your cup still empty?" Encourage use of the word *full*.
5. Ask the children to taste the water. Ask, "Is this ocean water? Is it salty?" Have them pour the drinking water into the sand.
6. Now fill their cups with salt water and repeat the concepts of "full" and "empty."
7. Have the children take a small sip of the salt water and ask, "How does it taste? Do we use water from the ocean as drinking water? Why not?" Ask the children to pour the water into the sand and offer fresh drinking water again to get the salty taste out of everyone's mouth.
8 Ask the children if drinking water makes the sand feel different from the way salt water makes it feel. Then allow the children free play in the sandbox.

Variations/Ways to Extend:

- Have the children compare sand with dirt. Ask, "How does each feel? Which is easier to dig a hole into? Which is more fun when mixed with water?"
- Read *What Did You Leave Behind?* by Alvin Tresselt (New York: Lothrop, 1978).

II–180 SAILBOATS GOOD ENOUGH TO EAT

Subject Area: Nutrition and Food Experience

Concepts/Skills: Understands prepositions
Plays using symbols
Develops fine motor movement

Objective: The children will create a sailboat out of celery and toothpicks.

Materials:
- Celery stalks
- Whipped cream cheese
- Spoons
- Scissors
- Knife
- Glue
- Toothpicks
- White paper

Procedure:

1. Throughout this activity, be sure to teach the following prepositions as the children are preparing the food and playing: *top, bottom, under, on.*

2. Wash the celery and cut each stalk into three- to four-inch pieces. Create sails by cutting white paper and gluing it to one side of each toothpick.

3. Have the children wash their hands. Distribute one piece of celery to each child.

4. Have each child fill the celery with whipped cream cheese.

5. Now distribute one sail to each child and let the children stand them up in the cream cheese.

6. Encourage the children to engage in symbolic play, pretending to sail their boats on a lake.

7. Conclude the activity by having the children eat the snacks.

8. When the children have finished eating, sing the following song to the tune of "Farmer in the Dell":

> Boats sail on water, Boats sail on water,
> Hi Ho the Derry-O, Boats sail on water.
> Today we ate our boats, Today we ate our boats,
> Hi Ho the Derry-O, Today we ate our boats.

Variations/Ways to Extend:

- Use pieces of wood as boats. Drill holes and place small wooden dowels with white cloth or white paper glued on for sails.
- Recite the poem "At the Seaside" by Robert Louis Stevenson.

AT THE SEASIDE

When I was down beside the sea My holes were empty like a cup.
A wooden spade they gave to me In every hole the sea came up.
To dig the sandy shore. Till it could come no more.

II–181   MISSING INSECT

Subject Area: Thinking Games

Concept/Skill: Recalls objects visually presented

Objectives: The children will identify insects and recall the picture that is missing.

Material: • Pictures

Procedure:

1. Using six pictures of various insects (ladybug, butterfly, ant, bee, dragonfly, and mosquito), play the "Missing Insect" game. Pictures of insects and spiders can be obtained by writing to:

   National Audubon Society
   950 Third Avenue
   New York, NY 10022
   (212) 832-3200
   Society for Visual Education
   1345 Diversey Parkway
   Chicago, IL 60614

2. Identify each insect and use the pictures to elicit certain facts from the children about insects. (All have six legs, some are harmful, and some are helpful.)

3. Select one child at a time and place three pictures on a table. After the child identifies the pictures (with help if necessary), ask him or her to close his or her eyes. Take one picture away and ask the child to indicate which picture was taken away.

4. Mix the pictures for each child and increase to four pictures when appropriate.

Variation/Way to Extend:

• Arrange an insect scavenger hunt. Hide the pictures in different places in the classroom. Ask the children to find them and identify each one.

II-182 LADYBUG

Subject Area: Language Arts

Concept/Skill: Memorizes simple rhyme

Objectives: The children will identify a ladybug and act out a simple rhyme about ladybugs.

Materials:
- Picture
- Words to rhyme

Procedure:

1. Show the children a picture of a ladybug. Emphasize that the ladybug helps farmers by eating insects that may hurt our fruits and vegetables.
2. Have the children repeat and act out the following rhyme. Begin by asking the children to stand several feet from one another:

   Ladybug, ladybug, (*move fingers*)
   Let me see your crawl. (*crawl slowly on all fours*)
   Hurry after those harmful bugs (*move quickly on all fours*)
   But be careful, do not fall! (*fall over*)

3. Repeat this rhyme several times.

Variations/Ways to Extend:

- Ask each child to recall the words and act out the poem.
- Recite the poem "Song of the Bugs" by Margaret W. Brown, found in her book *Nibble, Nibble* (Reading, MA: Addison-Wesley, 1959).

II–183   LOOKING AT INSECTS

Subject Area: Science

Concept/Skill: Observes objects closely

Objective: The children will closely observe live insects with a magnifying glass.

Materials:
- Insects in jars
- Magnifying glasses
- Magazine pictures

Procedure:

1. Bring in several jars containing insects you have caught. When looking for insects, such as grasshoppers, ants, and crickets, scoop them up with a jar and cover it with nylon and a rubber band.

2. Show the children a magnifying glass and demonstrate how it works by looking through it at magazine pictures.
3. Have the children examine each insect with the magnifying glass (one for every four children). Ask the children to describe the insects' movement and physical features (shape, color, size).
4. Identify each insect for the children. Put leaves in the jars as food.
5. After a day or two of captivity, take each insect outside and let the children observe their release.

Variations/Ways to Extend:

- Use the magnifying glass to look at pictures of insects. You might also have the children inspect such other items as flowers, leaves, and rocks.
- A lovely, simple song about the balance of nature is "Black-Eyed Susan" on *Songs of Nature and the Environment* by G. Axelrod and R. Macklin (Folkways Records, 632 Broadway, New York, NY 10012).

II–184   MOVING INSECTS

Subject Area: Creative Dramatics and Movement

Concepts/Skills: Moves body in response to simple teacher commands
Hops on one foot two or more times

Objectives: The children will pretend that they are insects and engage in creative dramatics by following the teacher's suggestions.

Materials: • Large open area
• Construction-paper headbands

Procedure:

1.   Have the children create paper headbands with antennae to look like insects. Tell the children to flap their arms for wings.

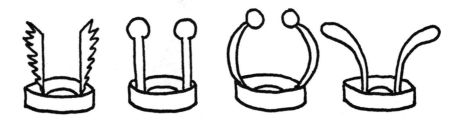

2.   Give the following directions to the children, allowing them to pretend they are insects and move their bodies creatively:

Pretend you are an insect. You have wings and six legs
and you are chasing a small fly.
Grab a small fly and let it go.
Show everyone your antennae by shaking your head.
"Buzz" like a bee.
Pretend you are an insect in water. Let's see you swim.
You are an insect that likes to hop. Hop three times.
Hop on one foot three times.
Move your nose as if you smelled something funny.
Fly to a flower.
Smell the flower. It smells so good.
Flap your arm. Flap both arms.
Shake your whole body.
Fly away under a tree and fall asleep.

Variations/Ways to Extend:

- To give the children wings, use a piece of sheer fabric, 36″ long and 20″ wide, and pin it to the child's cuffs and behind the collar.

- For background music during this activity, play a recording of "The Bee" by Schubert, available from RCA Victor Basic Record Library for Elementary Schools, 72 Fifth Avenue, New York, NY 10011.

- Teach this fingerplay to the children:

  Here is the beehive (*make a beehive with two hands and connect fingers*)
  But where are the bees?
  Hiding where nobody sees.
  Watch them come creeping
  Out of their hive.
  One, two, three, four, five, (*creep fingers of one hand out of the other, making them fly about*)
  > Buzz, gotcha!

II–185   GELATIN LADYBUG

Subject Areas: Math and Cooking Experience

Concepts/Skills: Rote counts
Understands number concepts

Objectives: The children will demonstrate counting and one-to-one correspondence while making a gelatin dessert.

Materials:
- Pot
- Heating source
- Book
- One small pie tin for each child
- Raisins
- Refrigerator
- Spoons
- 4 cups water
- 4 envelopes of unflavored gelatin
- 3 envelopes of cherry-flavored gelatin
- Licorice strings

Procedure:

1. Read *The Grouchy Ladybug* by Eric Carle (New York: Harper and Row, 1977) as a stimulus for this activity.
2. Tell the children that they are going to help make ladybugs that they will be able to eat.
3. Measure four cups of water into a pot and boil. (**Caution:** Be sure that the children stay away from the heat.) Add the envelopes of unflavored gelatin and the cherry-flavored gelatin, stirring until the mixture is dissolved. Pour the gelatin into the small individual tins. Let each child count out six raisins and place them in his or her gelatin for the ladybug's spots and add licorice strings for antennae. Refrigerate the gelatin ladybugs for one hour.

4. Let the children enjoy their gelatin ladybugs at snack time.

Variations/Ways to Extend

- Have each child draw his or her own version of a ladybug at the easel using tempera paints.
- Teach the following fingerplay to the children:

> One, two, three (*raise one finger at a time*)
> There's a bug on me. (*point to imaginary bug on knee*)
> Brush it away, (*make sweeping motion*)
> Where did it go? (*appear surprised*)
> I don't know! (*hold palms upward and shake head*)

II-186 NIGHTTIME CARDS

Subject Areas: Social Studies, Creative Drama, and Math

Concepts/Skills: Acts out simple everyday activities
Determines sequence of three pictured events
Engages in simple conversation

Objectives: The children will recall routines that they engage in at night, perform dramatizations of them, and place in sequence cards depicting these routines.

Materials: • Sequence cards (three to a set)

Procedure:

1. Discuss with the children some of the routines common to most of them at night, such as eating dinner, changing into pajamas, washing and brushing teeth, and being read a story.

2. Help a few children at a time organize their thoughts about one of these procedures and then dramatize it or act it out before the others. Do this with all the topics you have designated, keeping them simple and in easily definable steps.

3. Have the children take turns ordering a series of three cards you have made that depict the activity. For example, one set of cards might show people setting the table, eating dinner, and then cleaning up. A second set might show them going into the bedroom, putting on pajamas, and getting into bed. You might want to color code the backs of these cards to keep the sets distinct.

Variations/Ways to Extend:

• Teach the following nursery rhyme to the children:

> Hey, Diddle, Diddle! The cat and the fiddle,
> The cow jumped over the moon.
> The little dog laughed, to see such sport,
> And the dish ran away with the spoon.

• Read *The Moon & the Balloon* by Mike Thaler (New York: Hastings, 1982).

II-187 MUSICAL STARS

Subject Area: Gross Motor Games

Concepts/Skills: Listens for musical cues
Describes a picture

Objectives: The children will move to various pictures when cued by a recording and then describe what they see.

Materials:
- Record player
- Records of outer space movie themes
- Laminated pictures of the sun, moon, and stars
- Tape

Procedure:

1. Tape the pictures onto the floor in a wide circle. Include actual magazine photos or NASA photos. Write to:

    Educator's Resource Library NASA
    John F. Kennedy Space Center
    Florida 32899

2. Ask the children to walk around the circle while you play the records.
3. When the music stops, have the children stop walking and ask each to stand on a different picture. In turn, have the children tell what they see in their picture and how it tells something about day or night.
4. Continue until each child has had a turn describing a different picture.

Variations/Ways to Extend:

- Use the pictures for math readiness exercises. Count the number of pictures that show a sun or a moon, count the points on a star, and so on.
- Read *Wait Till the Moon Is Full* by Margaret W. Brown (New York: Harper and Row, 1948).

II-188 MOON PICTURES

Subject Area: Art

Concepts/Skills: Explores new technique
Expresses self creatively
Develops fine motor movement of squeezing an eyedropper

Objective: The children will observe by creating marble paintings how a round object can roll.

Materials:
- Shirt box for each child
- 5 marbles for each child
- Eyedropper for each child
- Tempera paints
- Paper cut to fit the boxes

Procedure:

1. Discuss the idea with the children that the moon is not flat, as it may appear to them, but rather is round, like a ball or a marble. Explain that it is bright at night because the moon catches light from the sun.
2. Ask each child to place a piece of paper in a shirt box.
3. Help the children to use the eyedroppers to draw up the color of tempera they want and drop some paint onto the paper.
4. Then have the children place their marbles in the boxes, close the lids, and then shake the boxes so that the marbles roll around and spread the paint.
5. When they are dry, display the moon pictures at the children's eye-level.

Variations/Ways to Extend:

- Let the children color a nighttime picture by pressing hard and coloring a small piece of heavy white paper with different crayon colors. Then have them color the whole sheet of paper with black crayon. Ask the children to then use toothpicks to etch a design through the black crayon.
- Let the children paint white or yellow stars on a big sheet of black or purple paper and then dust each one with silver glitter.
- Read the Caldecott Medal book *Many Moons* by James Thurber (San Diego, CA: Harcourt Brace Jovanovich, 1943).

II–189   CAN YOU FIND THE PICTURE?

Subject Area: Language Arts

Concepts/Skills: Understands questions as indicated by relevant response
Listens to short stories
Observes details

Objectives: The children will look at the pictures in a story book and answer questions about what they see.

Material: • Book

Procedure:

1. Read *Happy Birthday, Moon* by Frank Asch (Englewood Cliffs, NJ: Prentice-Hall, 1982) to the children, either in small groups or individually.
2. After reading, make a statement that describes one of the pictures in the book, such as "In this picture, I see a bear in a canoe on the water, and in the sky is a big yellow moon." Then close the book and hand it to a child. Ask that child to find the page that you described.
3. Continue with other statements, such as, "I see a bear wearing a big black hat." Do not make statements that confuse the child by being applicable to more than one page.

Variations/Ways to Extend:

• Let a child describe a picture to you, close the book, and ask you to find the picture.
• Let the children paint at the easel using dark blue, gray, or black paint. Provide white or yellow paint and suggest painting a moon somewhere on their dark sky.

II-190   STAR COUNT

Subject Area: Math

Concept/Skill: Understands number concepts by associating a number with a given quantity of objects

Objective: The children will apply stars to a chart coinciding with the appropriate number.

Materials:
- Sheet of paper for each child
- Star stickers
- Marker

Procedure:

1. In discussing day and night, mention to the children how bright and hot the stars really are that they see up in the sky at night.
2. Tell the children that they are going to count and make a chart of some bright shiny stars. (Note: This activity can be done with each individual child or with a group by making a large chart on manila paper.)
3. Number a sheet of paper from 1 to 6 down the left side for each child.
4. Help each child stick the appropriate number of stars in a line next to each number. Be sure the rows are straight enough for the child to see that each number stands for one more star than the last, as shown here.

    1   ★
    2   ★★
    3   ★★★
    4   ★★★★
    5   ★★★★★
    6   ★★★★★★

Variation/Way to Extend:

- Play this star game: Cut out a large star and write the numerals from 1 to 10 in a random fashion all over it. Create a matching exercise by giving a child an envelope of number cutouts to match those on the star.

II–191 VACATION SHAPES

Subject Area: Math

Concept/Skills: Matches circle, square, and triangle shapes

Objective: The children will construct a vacation picture using circles, triangles, and squares.

Materials:
- Pre-cut shapes
- Construction paper
- Crayons
- Pictures
- Glue

Procedure:

1. Show pictures of various kinds of transportation (cars, trains, planes and ships) and discuss going on vacation using one of those modes of travel. Discuss how the sun, during the summer, makes the weather very warm.

2. Using pre-cut circles, squares, and triangles of varying sizes, have the children create a vacation picture. Some shape examples are a sun (one large circle and twelve small triangles) and a camper (two squares with small circles for wheels).

 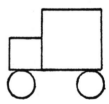

3. Ask the children to glue the shapes onto construction paper and color in other parts of the picture.

4. Using additional shapes, have the children match large and small circles, squares, and triangles.

Variations/Ways to Extend:
- Sing "You Are My Sunshine."
- Read *All Ready for Summer* by Leone Adelson (New York: McKay, 1956).

II–192 SUMMER ACTIVITIES

Subject Area: Creative Dramatics

Concept/Skill: Dramatizes common activities

Objective: The children will dramatize summertime activities.

Materials:
- Pictures
- Props and objects

Procedure:

1. Tell the children that they are going to dramatize summertime and vacation activities.
2. Using pictures, show the children examples of the following:
   swimming and water play
   swinging at a playground
   taking a walk
   riding a pony
   riding a tricycle
   picnicking
   boating
   collecting rocks and shells
   watching nature (flowers, butterflies, birds, ants)
   camping
   painting and coloring
   sightseeing, such as going to the zoo
3. Following a brief discussion of each activity, encourage the children to act out each activity. Provide props and objects for the children to use.

Variation/Way to Extend:

- Follow up this activity with a real experience, such as organizing and going on a picnic with the children.

II–193   COLORED SAND

Subject Area: Art

Concepts/Skills: Develops fine motor control
Becomes creative

Objective: The children will construct vacation sand pictures.

Materials: • Construction paper
• Glue
• Pre-cut shapes
• Powdered tempera paints
• Sand

Procedure:

1. Tell the children to close their eyes and see themselves enjoying a summer activity, such as swimming or picnicking. Then tell them they are going to design a picture of one of those summer activities using pre-cut paper items, glue, and colored sand (sand mixed with powdered tempera paint).

2. Distribute the pre-cut paper shapes of boats, shells, lakes, picnic tables, kites, and so on for the children to glue onto their papers to make scenes.

3. Help the children glue these paper scenes in place.

4. Then have the children spread glue over those areas of the picture that they want textured and sprinkle the colored sand over the glue. Shake off the excess sand after the glue dries.

5. Display the sand pictures on a wall area at the children's eye-level.

Variation/Way to Extend:

• Let each child give his or her picture a title and dictate to you a story about it.

II–194   ORANGE CREAM

Subject Area: Nutrition and Foods Experience

Concept/Skills: Demonstrates sense of smell and taste

Objectives: The children will participate in a foods experience by making and enjoying a cool summer drink together.

Materials: (this recipe makes four servings)
- 1 cup yogurt
- ½ orange, peeled and sliced
- ½ lemon, peeled and sliced
- 1 tablespoon lemon juice
- 1 tablespoon grated orange rind
- 2 tablespoons honey
- Blender
- Paper cups

Procedure:

1. Tell the children that they are going to learn how to make a special drink to help keep them cool this summer while they are at home or on vacation.
2. Combine the listed ingredients in a blender and mix until it is creamy.
3. Pour the orange cream into individual paper cups and let the children enjoy it for a snack.

Variation/Way to Extend:

- As the children enjoy their drinks, show them pictures of various settings (mountains, lakes, beaches, and resorts).

II-195 SUMMER PARTY

Subject Area: Social Studies

Concepts/Skills: Speaks in four- to six-word sentences
Feels good about self and abilities

Objectives: The children will engage in a party and create positive statements about themselves.

Materials:
- Large open space
- Pancake batter
- Cooking utensils
- Frying pan
- Fruit
- Markers
- Syrup
- Orange juice
- Paper cups
- Plates
- Forks
- Posterboard

Procedure:

1. Arrange a party to celebrate the arrival of summer and sunny days. Let the children move creatively by pretending to be balloons floating high in the sky or birds and butterflies flying toward the sun.
2. Prepare sun-shaped pancakes and serve them with fruit, syrup, and orange juice at snack time. (**Caution:** Be sure the children stay away from the heat when you prepare the pancakes.)
3. Help each child make a happy, positive affirmation about him- or herself and write this on posterboard for each child to decorate. Examples are "I am special because I like to paint with pink paint," "I work and play with my friends," and "I am growing up and am happy inside."
4. Display these statements on an exciting bulletin board.

Variation/Way to Extend:

- Celebrate the birthdays of all the children born during July and August if they will **not** be attending your class this summer.

APPENDIX

SPECIAL SECTION
FOR PRESCHOOL DIRECTORS

Directors who use the *Preschool Curriculum Activities Library* will have a strong rationale to support their choices of topics and activities with children of different ages. Those who have implemented this curriculum can easily demonstrate how activities dealing with the same topic can be developmentally different and therefore appropriate for children who vary in age.

Directors are often asked by parents of home-bound children if activities are available from the school that the parent can use at home to teach the child. Again, the learning experiences in this book can be offered to parents to reduce fears about their children "missing" a preschool experience.

As parents become more sophisticated regarding their choice of a preschool, they may ask to see the curriculum. Parents can be shown how themes and topics incorporate many different skills and age-appropriate experiences. Such a rationale provides a clear understanding of the school's direction and creates a sense of integration and purpose for children, parents, and staff.

At its best, curriculum development is an ongoing process. Therefore, modify the themes and daily activities to meet the local and geographic needs of your children. The changes made, however, will be within a coherent framework so that each child, starting at age two, will be able to build upon the skills and knowledge earlier gained.

Described below are six steps to follow when creating or improving a preschool curriculum. It is suggested that a team of teachers address the questions following each step. New learning experiences can be created that complement and support the activities found in the *Library,* providing a well-rounded curriculum based on a planned approach.

Step 1: DETERMINE BELIEFS ABOUT HOW CHILDREN LEARN

According to Jones (1981), there are two basic approaches to creating curriculum for young children:

Approach 1—create activities based on children's interests
Approach 2—create activitites based on what children need to know

Proponents of Approach #1 believe that preschool children learn through direct experience, in their own creative ways, using real, natural objects. Preschoolers are in what Jean Piaget (1952) has called the "preoperational stage"; they thrive on free choice and manipulation of concrete objects in a stimulating environment. Also, Approach #1 advocates believe that abstract language in young children is largely undeveloped and therefore teachers should keep verbalizations such as questions and conveyance of facts to a minimum.

Proponents of Approach #2, however, argue that a curriculum based on concrete experiences, with a minimum of teacher "talk", is difficult to justify. Instead, it is felt that children must be prepared for living in an American culture which places much importance on verbal skill and high test scores. Approach #2, therefore, places emphasis on teacher conveyance of information and development of the children's ability to recall that information.

The curriculum presented in the *Library* offers a *combination* of both approaches. Learning experiences have been devised that are of high interest to children and encourage them to construct, move, and interact, while providing teachers with the opportunity to communicate information in an appropriate manner. It is clear that preschool children need direct, concrete, and high-interest experiences along with well-timed guidance and instruction. A combination of both approaches is essential to building an effective preschool curriculum.

Questions for Teachers
1. Which approach does your school follow?
2. Are there enough concrete experiences?
3. Is there opportunity for teacher conveyance of information?
4. What changes should be made?

Step 2: SELECT LONG-RANGE GOALS FOR THE CHILDREN

Four long-range early childhood goals are listed below. The activities described in the *Library* are based on these goals.

- Competence—to develop children's ability in the areas of language, numbers, and interest in books
- Cooperation—to enhance *self-concept* and *other-concept* through group activity and sharing experiences
- Autonomy—to encourage children to initiate, ask questions, and make limited choices
- Creativity—to construct new products, think of new ideas, and find alternative solutions

Questions for Teachers
1. Are the learning experiences you've created directed at achieving the four goals?
2. Is each goal approached through a variety of activities?

Step 3: ASSESS CHILDREN'S SKILLS-CONCEPTS NEEDS

The foundation of preschool curriculum planning is the observation and assessment of the individual needs of children. The Skills-Concepts Checklist found in this book can be duplicated, placed in each child's folder, and used to evaluate his or her progress during January and June of the school year. Anecdotal comments can be added to a child's folder to assist teachers in determining the skills that he or she has learned or that need to be strengthened.

Questions for Teachers
1. Do you take enough time to observe each child and record significant observations?
2. Do you keep a file folder on each child, containing the Checklist and anecdotal information?

3. Do you use your observations to make curricular changes?
4. How can the Checklist be modified to reflect special skills appropriate to your population of children?

Step 4: CREATE DEVELOPMENTALLY APPROPRIATE ACTIVITIES

All of the activities described in the *Library* are designed to achieve the long-range goals stated in Step 2 and develop the competencies found in the Skills-Concepts Checklist. Each learning experience develops one or more skills or concepts and is related to one of the six general content areas deemed appropriate for preschool children by Hildebrand (1980):

- The Child (personal data; health; body parts; relationship to family, school, and the world)
- The Community (people, workers, institutions, traditions)
- World of Plants (beauty, food)
- World of Machines (vehicles, small machines)
- World of Animals (pleasure, food)
- Physical Forces in World (weather)

Each activity in the *Library* is categorized into one of the following subject areas:

Language Arts	Art
Science	Music
Nutrition/Foods Experience	Math
Creative Dramatics/Movement	Thinking Games
Social Studies	Gross Motor Games

The children's learning can be further enhanced through additional field trips; the creation of learning experiences; and the use of traditional preschool materials and equipment such as blocks, sand, water, and paint (Seefeldt, 1980). The activities should be implemented in a classroom environment that, according to Harms and Clifford (1980), contains four characteristics:

- *Predictable* (well-defined activity centers, noisy and quiet areas, and labeled items)
- *Supportive* (child-sized equipment, play-alone space, and self-selection in activities)
- *Reflective* (children's artwork displayed, and multicultural and nonsexist materials)
- *Varied* (balance of active and quiet times, and indoor and outdoor play)

Questions for Teachers
1. Can the activities created and implemented by the staff be justified based on age-appropriateness?
2. How can the activities, themes, and subthemes found in this book be modified to fit the interests and needs of your children?
3. Are learning centers appropriately equipped?
4. Is the class environment predictable, supportive, reflective, and varied?

Step 5: PLAN FOR REPETITION OF CONCEPTS

Skills and concepts learned by young children need to be reinforced and extended. Many early childhood experts agree that facts must be placed into a structural pattern or frame of reference; otherwise, they will be forgotten. The pattern of activities found in this curriculum follows the model of primary and secondary reinforcement as described by Harlan (1980).

Harlan believes that concepts are built slowly from many simple facts or instances that can be generalized into a unifying idea. She recommends that teachers use her idea of *primary reinforcement* by creating a variety of activities (stories, fingerplays, songs, art, creative movement, math, food experiences, and so on) and by consciously reinforcing a concept or skill throughout each learning experience.

The curriculum presented here allows children to study one topic each week and be exposed to one of the ten subject areas (listed in Step 4) each day. By creating five different activities around one topic, the teacher has the opportunity to reinforce and extend concepts and skills.

Questions for Teachers
1. Are skills and concepts learned in one activity reinforced in other activities?
2. Can further activities be created that reinforce existing learning experiences?

Step 6: EVALUATE THE CHILDREN'S PROGRESS

Teachers can effectively evaluate the success of each activity by reviewing each lesson's stated behavioral objective and concepts/skills to be learned. They can then ask the question, "To what extent did each child learn what we intended to be learned?" Anecdotal notes can be briefly written and the Checklist can be used regarding each child's demonstrated behavior and skill acquisition. Decisions can be made providing for individual assistance or creating a new activity to reinforce a skill that a child may have had difficulty acquiring.

Questions for Teachers
1. When will the staff take some time (immediately after an activity, before lunch, after school) to evaluate what the children have learned?
2. What provisions can be made to assist children in acquiring certain skills?

REFERENCES

Harlan, Jean, *Science Experiences for the Early Childhood Years*. Columbus, Ohio: Chas. E. Merrill, 1980.

Harms, Thelma, and Richard M. Clifford, *Early Childhood Environmental Rating Scale*. New York Teacher's College Press, 1980.

Hildebrand, Verna, *Introduction to Early Childhood Education*. Columbus, Ohio: Chas. E. Merrill, 1980.

Jones, Edwin, *Dimensions of Teaching-Learning Environments: Handbook for Teachers*. Pasadena, Calif.: Pacific Oaks College Press, 1981.

Piaget, Jean, *The Origins of Intelligence in Children*. New York: International Universities Press, 1952.

Seefeldt, Carol, *Teaching Young Children*. Englewood Cliffs, N.J.: Prentice-Hall, 1980.

COMPLETE PRESCHOOL
DEVELOPMENT PLAN

SKILLS-CONCEPTS CHECKLIST*
FOR TWO-YEAR-OLDS
(Developmental Characteristics)

A child who is 24 to 36 months of age tends to develop skills rapidly. The following abilities will emerge as the child approaches age three. The activities within this book have been designed to develop the skills and concepts listed below in a manner consistent with the child's needs and interests. Monitor the child's progress and evaluate it twice during the school year by placing a check (√) next to the skill or concept once it has been mastered.

Name _____ Birthdate _____

COGNITIVE

Personal Curiosity/Autonomy	JAN.	JUNE
1. Shows curiosity and interest in surroundings		
2. Imitates the actions of adults		
3. Imitates play of other children		
4. Finds own play area or activity		
5. Enjoys looking at books		
6. Begins to notice differences between safe and unsafe environments (2½ to 3)		

Senses		
7. Begins to develop senses of touch, smell, taste, and hearing		
8. Begins to place large puzzle pieces in appropriate slots		

Memory		
9. Refers to self by name		
10. Points to common object on command		
11. Associates use with common objects		
12. Stacks three rings by size		
13. Knows that different activities go on at different times of the day (2½ to 3)		
14. Understands the idea of waiting for someone else to go first (2½ to 3)		

Creativity		
15. Shows simple symbolic play (pretends block is a cup)		
16. Acts out a simple story (2½ to 3)		
17. Draws a face (no arms or legs) (2½ to 3)		

Comments:

_____

_____

_____

_____

* This Checklist was developed from the *Skill-Concept Development Checklists for Two Through Five Year Olds* (St. Louis County, Missouri: Parent-Child Early Education). Developed by the Ferguson-Florissant School District. Parts reprinted with their permission.

LANGUAGE

Sentence Structure	JAN.	JUNE
18. Describes what happened in two or three words		
19. Verbalizes wants ("Want water.")		
20. Repeats parts of songs, rhymes, and fingerplays		
21. Gives first and last names when asked (2½ to 3)		
22. Uses short sentences to convey simple ideas (2½ to 3)		

Listening

23. Listens to simple stories and songs		
24. Follows simple directions		
25. Places objects in, on, beside, or under		
26. Identifies loud and soft		

Labeling

27. Identifies own gender		
28. Identifies boy or girl		
29. Identifies self in mirror		
30. Names common objects in pictures		

Comments:

_____

_____

_____

_____

_____

SELF

31. Points to six body parts when named		
32. Puts on and removes coat unassisted		
33. Lifts and drinks from cup and replaces on table		
34. Spoon feeds without spilling		
35. Begins to understand cleanliness		
36. Helps put things away		

Comments:

_____

_____

_____

SOCIAL STUDIES

37. Identifies self from a snapshot		
38. Shows pleasure in dealing with people and things		
39. Values own property and names personal belongings (2½ to 3)		
40. Follows simple rules in a game run by an adult (2½ to 3)		

Comments:

_____

_____

_____

_____

MATH

Counting	JAN.	JUNE
41. Understands the concept of "one"		
42. Counts two (repeats two digits)		
43. Indicates awareness of more than two (2½ to 3)		

Classifying		
44. Groups things together by size (one category) (2½ to 3)		

Size Differences		
45. Points to big and little objects (2½ to 3)		

Shapes		
46. Differentiates circle and square (2½ to 3)		

Comments: _____

_____

_____

_____

SCIENCE (2½ to 3)

Concepts		
47. Knows the names of three animals		
48. Can associate the words *grass, plants,* and *trees* with correct objects		
49. Identifies rain, clouds, and sun		
50. Begins to understand hard and soft		
51. Begins to understand hot and cold		
52. Begins to understand wet and dry		
53. Matches two color samples		

Comments: _____

_____

_____

_____

GROSS MOTOR

Arm-Eye Coordination		
54. Throws a small object two feet		
55. Catches a rolled ball and rolls it forward		

Body Coordination		
56. Jumps with two feet		
57. Claps with music		
58. Walks on tip toe		
59. Walks upstairs alone (both feet on each step) (2½ to 3)		
60. Walks downstairs alone (both feet on each step) (2½ to 3)		
61. Hops on one foot (2½ to 3)		

Comments: _____

_____

_____

FINE MOTOR

Finger Strength and Dexterity	JAN.	JUNE
62. Fills and dumps containers with sand		
63. Turns single pages (2½ to 3)		

Eye-Hand Coordination		
64. Applies glue and pastes collage pieces		
65. Paints with a large brush		
66. Tears paper		
67. Strings five large beads		
68. Colors with a large crayon		
69. Rolls, pounds, and squeezes clay		
70. Draws a horizontal line		
71. Builds a six-block tower (2½ to 3)		
72. Uses scissors with one hand to cut paper (2½ to 3)		

Comments:

_____

_____

_____

_____

SKILLS-CONCEPTS CHECKLIST*
FOR THREE-YEAR-OLDS
(Developmental Characteristics)

A child who is 36 to 48 months of age continues to expand his or her cognitive, affective, and physical growth. The following abilities will emerge as the child approaches age four. The activities within this book have been designed to develop the skills and concepts listed below in a manner consistent with the child's needs and interests. Monitor the child's progress and evaluate it twice during the school year by placing a check (√) next to the skill or concept once it has been mastered.

Name _____ Birthdate _____

COGNITIVE

Personal Curiosity/Autonomy	JAN.	JUNE
1. Shows curiosity and the need to investigate/explore anything new		
2. Asks questions (Who?, What?, Where?, or Why?)		

Senses

3. Demonstrates accurate sense of touch, smell, and taste		
4. Identifies common sounds		
5. Places objects on their outlines		
6. Observes objects closely		

Memory

7. Recalls three objects that are visually presented		
8. Identifies what's missing from a picture		
9. Acts out simple everyday activities		

Logical Thinking

10. Places three pictured events from a familiar story in sequence and expresses each picture sequence in three thoughts		

Relationships

11. Pairs related objects and pictures, such as shoe and sock		
12. Recognizes which doesn't belong in a group of three items (for example, banana, chair, and apple)		

Creativity

13. Draws a face with facial parts and stick arms and legs		
14. Dramatizes a simple story		
15. Uses animistic thinking (stuffed animals have human characteristics)		
16. Plays using symbols (objects stand for real objects)		

Comments: _____

_____

* This checklist was developed from the *Skill-Concept Development Checklists for Two Through Five Year Olds* (St. Louis County, Missouri: Parent-Child Early Education). Developed by the Ferguson-Florissant School District. Parts reprinted with their permission.

LANGUAGE

Sentence Structure

	JAN.	JUNE
17. Speaks in four- to six-word sentences		
18. Uses *I, you, me, he,* and *she* correctly		
19. Engages in simple conversation		
20. Memorizes and repeats simple rhymes, songs, or fingerplays of four lines		
21. Understands sentences and questions as indicated by a relevant response		
22. Names plural form to refer to more than one		
23. Describes action in pictures		

Listening

	JAN.	JUNE
24. Listens to short stories and simple poems		
25. Follows two directions		
26. Understands opposites (up/down; open/closed; stop/go; happy/sad; fast/slow; hot/cold)		
27. Understands prepositions (in, out, over, under, on, off, top, bottom, in front of, in back of)		

Labeling

	JAN.	JUNE
28. Names concrete objects in environment		
29. Recognizes and names articles of clothing worn		
30. Recognizes and names pieces of furniture		

Comments:

_____

_____

_____

SELF

	JAN.	JUNE
31. Points to and names body parts (head, hands, arms, knees, legs, chin, feet, and face parts)		
32. Tells own full name, sex, and age		
33. Feels good about self and abilities		

Comments:

_____

_____

_____

SOCIAL STUDIES

Interpersonal

	JAN.	JUNE
34. Enjoys being with other children		
35. Begins learning the give and take of play		
36. Begins participation in a group		

Concepts

	JAN.	JUNE
37. Begins to understand that self and others change		
38. Understands that parental figures care for home and family		
39. Understands that people are alike and different in how they look and feel (3½ to 4)		

Comments:

_____

_____

_____

MATH

Counting

	JAN.	JUNE
40. Rote counts to ten		
41. Understands number concepts (when presented with a given number of objects, child can tell how many there are up to six)		

Classifying

42. Sorts objects into two given categories (by size, shape, or color)		

Size Differences

43. Understands concepts of full and empty		
44. Understands big/little; tall/short		

Shapes

45. Points to and labels shapes		
46. Matches shapes (circle, square, triangle, and rectangle)		

Sets

47. Matches sets containing up to five objects		
48. Constructs sets of blocks when given a model		

Comments: _____
_____
_____
_____

SCIENCE

Concepts

49. Understands that there are many kinds of animals		
50. Understands that animals move in different ways		
51. Understands that most plants make seeds for new plants		
52. Understands that seeds grow into plants with roots, stems, leaves, and flowers		
53. Understands that air is everywhere		
54. Understands that water has weight		

Colors

55. Matches colors		
56. Points to appropriate color upon command		
57. Names three primary colors (red, yellow, and blue)		

Comments: _____
_____
_____
_____

GROSS MOTOR

Arm–Eye Coordination

58. Catches a large ball from 5- to 8-foot distance		
59. Throws a ball overhand with accuracy from 4- to 6-foot distance		
60. Rolls a large ball to a target		
61. Throws a beanbag at a target five feet away		

Body Coordination	JAN.	JUNE
62. Walks forward/backward on an 8-foot line		
63. Jumps three jumps with both feet		
64. Hops on one foot two or more times		
65. Moves body in response to simple teacher commands		
66. Walks on tiptoe		
67. Rides a tricycle		
68. Claps with music		

Comments: _____

_____

_____

_____

FINE MOTOR

Finger Strength and Dexterity

	JAN.	JUNE
69. Makes balls and snakes with clay		
70. Pastes with index finger		

Eye-Hand Coordination

	JAN.	JUNE
71. Strings at least four half-inch beads		
72. Puts pegs into pegboard		
73. Screws and unscrews nuts, bolts, and lids of various sizes		
74. Holds crayon with fingers rather than fist		
75. Paints with a large brush on large piece of paper		
76. Copies horizontal lines, vertical lines, circles, crosses, diagonal lines		
77. Uses scissors but does not necessarily follow lines		
78. Puts together a six- or seven-piece puzzle		
79. Laces following a sequence of holes		

Comments: _____

_____

_____

_____

SKILLS–CONCEPTS CHECKLIST*
FOR FOUR-YEAR-OLDS
(Developmental Characteristics)

A child who is 48 to 60 months of age typically demonstrates a large increase in vocabulary and physical abilities. The following abilities will emerge as the child approaches age five. The activities within this book have been designed to develop the skills and concepts listed below in a manner consistent with the child's needs and interests. Monitor the child's progress and evaluate it twice during the school year by placing a check (√) next to the skill or concept once it has been mastered.

Name _____ Birthdate _____

COGNITIVE

Personal Curiosity/Autonomy	JAN.	JUNE
1. Shows an increasing curiosity and sense of adventure		
2. Asks an increasing number of questions		
3. Takes initiative in learning		
4. Shows an interest in the printed word		
5. Pays attention and concentrates on a task		

Senses		
6. Demonstrates accurate sense of touch ("thick" or "thin") and smell		
7. Describes foods by taste (sweet, sour, and salty)		
8. Reproduces a simple pattern of different items from memory		
9. Ranks sounds (loud, louder, loudest; soft, softer, softest)		
10. Observes objects and pictures closely		

Memory		
11. Recalls information previously taught		

Logical Thinking		
12. Interprets the main idea of a story		
13. Orders pictures by time sequence to tell a story		

Relationships		
14. Makes a simple comparison of two objects in terms of difference ("How are a cat and dog different?") and sameness ("How are a cat and dog alike?")		
15. Completes a statement of parallel relationships		

Predicting		
16. Predicts what will happen next in a story or situation		
17. Predicts realistic outcomes of events ("What will happen if we go on a picnic?")		

* This checklist was developed from the *Skill–Concept Development Checklists for Two Through Five Year Olds* (St. Louis County, Missouri: Parent–Child Early Education). Developed by the Ferguson–Florissant School District. Parts reprinted with their permission.

Creativity

	JAN.	JUNE
18. Responds well to nondirective questions ("How many ways can you think of to move across the room?")		
19. Proposes alternative ways of doing art experiences, movement activities, and story endings		
20. Represents thoughts in pictures		
21. Draws a human figure with major body parts		
22. Participates verbally or nonverbally in imaginative play or puppetry (socio-dramatic play)		
23. Acts out a familiar story or nursery rhyme as the teacher recites		

Comments:

_____

_____

_____

LANGUAGE

Sentence Structure

	JAN.	JUNE
24. Speaks in six, eight, ten, or more words		
25. Makes relevant verbal contributions in small group discussion		
26. Shows understanding of past, present, and future tenses by using proper verb form		
27. Verbalizes songs and fingerplays		
28. Dictates own experience stories		
29. Describes a simple object using color, size, shape, composition, and use		
30. Describes a picture with three statements		

Listening

	JAN.	JUNE
31. Listens to directions for games and activities		
32. Listens to stories of at least ten minutes in length		
33. Retells five-sentence short story in sequence using own words		
34. Understands prepositions		

Labeling

	JAN.	JUNE
35. Labels common everyday items such as clothing, animals, and furniture		
36. Orally labels pictures and drawings ("That's a dog.")		

Letter/Word Recognition

	JAN.	JUNE
37. Verbally identifies letters in first name (and subsequently in last name)		
38. Identifies many letters of the alphabet		
39. Distinguishes words that begin with the same sound (*book/boy*)		
40. Names two words that rhyme in a group of three (*tie, road, pie*)		
41. Supplies a rhyming word to rhyme with a word given by the teacher		
42. Associates a letter with its sound in spoken words		

Comments:

_____

_____

_____

_____

SELF	JAN.	JUNE
43. Touches, names, and tells function of parts of the body (head, eyes, hands, arms, feet, legs, nose, mouth, ears, neck, trunk, ankle, knee, shoulder, wrist, elbow, and heel)		
44. Verbalizes full name, address, age, birthday, and telephone number		
45. Identifies expressions of feelings		
46. Feels good about self and abilities		

Comments: _____

_____

_____

SOCIAL STUDIES

Interpersonal

	JAN.	JUNE
47. Shows empathy toward other children		
48. Works cooperatively with adults		
49. Works and plays cooperatively with other children		

Concepts

	JAN.	JUNE
50. Begins to understand that problems can be solved by talking and not fighting		
51. Understands that we wear appropriate clothing to protect us from extremes of weather		
52. Understands that families share responsibilities of work and recreation		
53. Begins to understand the importance of keeping the school surroundings clean and free from litter		

Comments: _____

_____

_____

MATH

Counting

	JAN.	JUNE
54. Counts from 1 to _____		
55. Understands ordinal positions first through fifth		
56. Recognizes and orders the cardinal numerals in sequence		
57. Solves simple verbal problems using numerals ("If you have two pieces of candy and I give you one more, how many will you have?")		

Classifying

	JAN.	JUNE
58. Classifies objects by color, size, shape, and texture		

Size Differences

	JAN.	JUNE
59. Orders and compares size differences (big, bigger, biggest; small, smaller, smallest; short, shorter, shortest; long, longer, longest)		

Shapes

	JAN.	JUNE
60. Points to and names: triangle, circle, square, rectangle, and diamond		

	JAN.	JUNE
Quantitative Concepts		
61. Distinguishes between concepts of "some," "most," and "all"		
62. Compares objects as to weight ("Which is heavier?" "Which is lighter?")		
63. Understands concepts of "full," "half full," and "empty"		
64. Understands fractions (½, ¼, whole)		
Sets		
65. Identifies a set as a collection of objects having a common property		
66. Establishes a one-to-one correspondence through matching members of equivalent sets (matching six cowboys to six cowboy hats)		
67. Distinguishes between equivalent and non-equivalent sets through matching		
68. Understands that each number is one more than the preceding number ("What is one more than two?")		
69. Identifies an empty set as one having no members		

Comments: _____

_____

_____

SCIENCE

Concepts		
70. Understands that each animal needs its own kind of food and shelter		
71. Understands that plants need water, light, warmth, and air to live		
72. Understands that many foods we eat come from seeds and plants		
73. Understands that some things float in water and some things sink in water		
74. Understands the balance of nature—that is, animals need to eat plants, vegetables, and insects in order to live		
75. Understands that plant life, animal life, and other aspects of the environment must be respected		
Colors		
76. Points to and names colors		

Comments: _____

_____

_____

GROSS MOTOR

Arm-Eye Coordination		
77. Catches a ball away from body with hands only (large ball/small ball)		
78. Throws a ball or beanbag with direction		
79. Throws a ball into the air and catches it by self		
80. Bounces and catches a ball		

Body Coordination

	JAN.	JUNE
81. Walks forward and backward on a line ten feet long without stepping off		
82. Walks a line heel-to-toe eight feet long without stepping off		
83. Balances on foot for five seconds		
84. Stops movement activity upon teacher's direction		
85. Moves body creatively upon teacher's direction		
86. Claps with music		

Rhythm

87. Claps and marches in time with music		
88. Responds to rhythms with appropriate body movements		

General Movement

89. Produces the following motions: walks backwards, runs smoothly, marches, skips, gallops, hops four times on each foot, walks heel-to-toe, and walks and runs on tiptoe		

Comments: _____

_____

_____

_____

FINE MOTOR

Finger Strength and Dexterity

90. Folds and creases paper two times		
91. Folds paper into halves, quarters, and diagonals		

Eye-Hand Coordination

92. Strings ten small beads		
93. Follows a sequence of holes when lacing		
94. Works a puzzle of ten or more pieces		
95. Uses crayon or pencil with control within a defined area		
96. Connects a dotted outline to make a shape		
97. Follows a series of dot-to-dot numerals, 1–10, to form an object		
98. Reproduces shapes (circle, square, triangle, and rectangle)		
99. Controls brush and paint		
100. Uses scissors with control to cut along a straight line and a curved line		

Comments: _____

_____

_____

_____